Accelerated Learning.
The Most Effective Techniques:
How to Learn Fast, Improve Memory, Save Your Time and Be Successful

Positive Psychology Coaching Series

Copyright © 2017 by Ian Tuhovsky

Author's blog: www.mindfulnessforsuccess.com
Author's Amazon profile: amazon.com/author/iantuhovsky
Instagram profile: https://instagram.com/mindfulnessforsuccess

All rights reserved. No part of this publication may be reproduced, stored in a retrieval system, or transmitted, in any form or by any means, electronic, mechanical, photocopying, recording or otherwise without the prior written permission of the author and the publishers.

The scanning, uploading, and distribution of this book via the Internet, or via any other means, without the permission of the author is illegal and punishable by law.

Please purchase only authorized electronic editions, and do not participate in or encourage electronic piracy of copyrighted materials.

Important

The book is not intended to provide medical advice or to take the place of medical advice and treatment from your personal physician. Readers are advised to consult their own doctors or other qualified health professionals regarding the treatment of medical conditions. The author shall not be held liable or responsible for any misunderstanding or misuse of the information contained in this book. The information is not indeed to diagnose, treat or cure any disease.

It's important to remember that the author of this book is not a doctor/therapist/medical professional. Only opinions based upon his own personal experiences or research are cited. The author does not offer medical advice or prescribe any treatments. For any health or medical issues – you should be talking to your doctor first.

Please be aware that every e-book and "short read" I publish is truly written by me, with thoroughly researched content 100% of the time. Unfortunately, there's a huge number of low quality, cheaply outsourced spam titles on Kindle non-fiction market these days, created by various Internet marketing companies. **I don't tolerate these books. I want to provide you with high quality, so** if you think that one of my books/short reads can be improved in some way, please contact me at:

contact@mindfulnessforsuccess.com

I will be very happy to hear from you, because you are who I write my books for!

Chapter 1: Accelerated Learning & Memorization Techniques – The Ultimate Keys To Success 4

Chapter 2: Setting Yourself Up For Success: How Your Attitude & Lifestyle Affect Your Learning .. 10

Chapter 3. How To Absorb Information Rapidly: Learning To Read More Quickly Than You Ever Thought Possible 16

Chapter 4: How To Learn By Listening 21

Chapter 5: Organizing Information: How To Take Notes That Get Results 25

Chapter 6: The Fastest Way To Test Your Knowledge: The Feynman Technique 30

Chapter 7: Learning By Experience & Reflection: Experiential Learning 34

Chapter 8: The Killer Strategy That Separates The Best Students From The Rest Of The Class 39

Chapter 9: How To Use Flashcards Effectively 44

Chapter 10: Spaced Repetition: How To Realize The Full Potential Of Flashcards 49

Chapter 11: Music, Binaural Beats, & Learning 53

Chapter 12: How To Beat Procrastination & Get Down To Work Fast 58

Chapter 13: The Truth About Learning Styles 63

Chapter 14: How To Master Mind Mapping 68

Chapter 15: Powerful Mnemonic Systems That Work 73

Chapter 16: The Method Of Loci 79

Chapter 17: Environmental Context & Cues – Are They Important Factors In Your Learning? 85

Chapter 18: Interleaved Practice – How To Polish Your Skills Quickly 91

Chapter 19: Accelerated Learning As Part Of A Group 96

Chapter 20: How To Cram Before An Exam 103

Chapter 21: How To Learn A Language Fast 108

Chapter 22: Social Learning – How To Remember Names & Faces 114

Chapter 23: Conclusion 118

    My Free Gift to You – Get One of My Audiobooks For Free! 121

Recommended Reading for You 123

About The Author 137

Chapter 1: Accelerated Learning & Memorization Techniques – The Ultimate Keys To Success

The human brain is an amazing organ. Comprised of over 100 billion nerve cells and 1,000 trillion synaptic connections, it can process a vast amount of information.[1] No wonder we are so good at learning new skills and absorbing so much knowledge. You might not think you are especially intelligent or "good at learning," but consider how much you have already learned over the course of your life to date.

Within a few hours of your birth, you learned what your parents smelled like, and how to imitate the facial expressions of other people. Within your first year, you learned how to sit up, how to crawl, and you began to learn how to walk. Later, you learned how to use language. The fact that you can read the words on this page testifies to the astonishing powers of the human brain. No other animal on earth has such a high level of cognitive ability.

Given that every individual is a learning machine, why do so many of us lose faith in our abilities by the time we reach adulthood? Of course, the information we have to learn as adolescents and adults is more complex and abstract than that which we had to learn as children. As a result, it makes sense that we are more likely to experience setbacks and failure, and this can have a negative effect on our confidence. For example, most people would say that learning how to tackle algebraic equations is harder than learning how to crawl along the floor. However, there's more to the story. The simple fact is that most of us know what we have to learn, but we don't know how to learn it! We may start off determined to grow our knowledge in a particular area, but quickly give up when we don't see quick results.

Worse, some of us come to see ourselves as inadequate or even stupid, and abandon our dreams altogether. Fortunately, once you master the techniques used by the world's best learners, you will tap into your brain's full potential. Difficult concepts will seem so much simpler, and you will feel inspired to grow your knowledge day by day. There is no reason why you cannot become a high achiever. All you need to do is give your learning style an overhaul, and commit to trying new methods of assimilating knowledge.

---

[1] Mastin, L. (2010). *Neurons & Synapses.* http://www.human-memory.net/brain_neurons.html

You may feel somewhat skeptical at this point. These ideas may go against everything you have ever been told about learning. As children and teens, we were taught that in order to learn new skills, we must work hard and hope that they somehow "sink in." The problem is, we are not told how or why some learning techniques are better than others, and we are left to our own devices when it comes to finding out what works for us.

We are also taught that some people are intrinsically "better" at accumulating knowledge, an illusion which is furthered by the school grading system. Those who receive B grades come to believe that they are less intelligent than those who get As. Our childhood experiences have a significant impact on our self-image, so these beliefs can be damaging. A child who decides that they are not as competent as their peers will carry that belief into adulthood. Many Western schools have begun to use more interactive teaching styles over the past couple of decades, but many of us still carry these old assumptions with us.

If you have ever struggled to understand a concept whilst watching a classmate or colleague absorb it with no apparent effort, you may have concluded that they are simply smarter than you. It is true that some people are indeed more intelligent than others. If this weren't the case, the whole notion of IQ would make no sense. Some people do achieve higher scores on tests of intelligence. However, in most real-world scenarios, a few extra IQ points doesn't really explain the difference between high and average performance.

At school, I was a capable student. I got good grades, and then went on to enjoy a successful college career. However, I rarely got perfect scores on my tests, and often had the feeling that I wasn't quite living up to my potential. During my second year of college, I watched my roommate Scott ace class after class. Chemistry, physics, math – he could do it all! I won't lie – Scott was a good friend, but I started to feel a little jealous. What really infuriated me was that, of the two of us, I spent more time studying every week. I assumed that he must have been gifted with the brain of a genius and the motivation of a world-class athlete.

One day, I swallowed my pride and asked him what it was like to be so naturally smart. I was curious what it felt like to sail through even advanced classes, and was eager to hear his answer. However, his response shocked me. "Well," Scott said, "I mean, you just practice. Get it done. But don't forget to have some fun too. It's how my parents always taught me to approach my schoolwork. I guess it just stuck." This conversation prompted me to research the science of learning and memory. It was hard work – there is a lot of misinformation out there – but I was thrilled to discover that anyone can improve their memory and study skills. I started achieving higher grades, and my new understanding of learning and memory has served me well in the workplace. I was able to keep abreast of new developments in my field, because my reading and retention abilities improved. In my spare time I started learning a couple of foreign languages, and became fluent within a couple of years.

I do not consider myself "special," just someone who had the good fortune to learn a set of tips and tricks relatively early on in life. Star performers not only identify what they need to learn, but they also know exactly how to learn it. They know that there is no point in turning up to lectures, reading books, or attending training programs, unless you have the right strategies in place that will help you absorb new skills and information.

This doesn't mean, however, that your superstar classmate or knowledgeable co-worker will necessarily teach you how to learn. They may have hit upon a great strategy by chance early in life, and just know that it works. This does not mean that they know how to teach others. Second, some people are naturally competitive, and even if they could articulate exactly how they learn, they might not want to share what they regard as their secret weapon. Finally, there are many accelerated learning techniques out there. Whilst every technique will work for some people, it won't work for everyone. Even if you happened to come across a super-learner who is willing and able to share their strategies, they may not work for you. This might even leave you feeling somewhat discouraged.

That's where this book comes in. I wrote it for everyone who wants to learn in a more efficient manner, but isn't sure where to start. You will learn numerous techniques that will enable you to pick up new knowledge at a faster rate than you ever dreamed possible. If you are in school or college, the advantages are obvious. You will be able to waste less time when preparing for exams, and you will feel more confident about your academic ability in general. This will boost your self-esteem, which will motivate you further, which will build on your existing success, and so on.

If you are in the workplace, you will also benefit from the techniques in this book. We are living in an age whereby knowledge and creativity are crucial commodities that anyone looking to gain respect within their field needs to develop. Unfortunately, we also lead busy lives, and it's hard to make time to read and retain knowledge found in books and articles. We need to make sure that we use our time efficiently. **Accelerated learning methods allow us to do just that.**

You will quickly develop a reputation as an expert in your field. You will learn how to read and absorb information at lightning speed, which will set you apart from your competitors. When you go to conferences, you will be able to take high-quality notes that enable you to review the material at a later date.

You will also benefit from these techniques if you are a parent. Nowadays, children and teens are encouraged to get involved in "hands-on" learning in school. Understanding the rationale behind these developments will allow you to better support your child. When they take part in projects or have to run experiments in class, you will already know why and how their teachers are taking this approach to learning. This will help you feel confident in taking an active role in your child's education.

It doesn't matter whether you are a teen, a senior citizen, or somewhere in between. It doesn't matter whether you are male or female, a PhD graduate or someone who didn't get the chance to complete high school. All you need is an open mind and a positive attitude. Accelerated learning is accessible to all. There are still plenty of myths about learning and age in circulation. "You can't teach an old dog new tricks" is, in my opinion, one of the most annoying and harmful sayings out there! It's true that your brain is more adaptable and plastic in your youth, but it keeps on developing throughout your life.

Another important issue we will look at in this book is motivation. **The notion that the most successful learners are not only highly intelligent, but also highly motivated, is simply wrong.** The truth is that no-one feels motivated to study all the time. Learning a new skill or developing an in-depth understanding of a topic takes time, it requires effort, and it may entail overcoming setbacks. It is natural to feel like slacking off occasionally. High achievers know that it is pointless to sit around and wait until they feel motivated to do something. In this book, you will learn the truth about motivation, momentum, and procrastination. **There are several practical techniques you can start using today that will greatly increase**

your output.

In fact, I've placed a general emphasis on methods and actionable tips throughout the book. From setting up your lifestyle in such a way that supports learning, to highly specific techniques for remembering names and faces, this guide will help you apply the science of learning to any situation. There are lots of books on learning available for you to buy, but most contain broad, generalized advice such as, "Don't leave learning to the last minute!" and "Take good notes!" These tips are all well and good, but they aren't going to help you get results. You need step-by-step instructions and high-quality information that will help you make the most of your time, and I'm happy to say that this book will provide you with exactly that!

The first couple of chapters address the adjustments that you will need to make in terms of your mindset and lifestyle. If you don't optimize your sleep and nutritional intake, your ability to learn will suffer. Think of these chapters as groundwork for the methods you are about to learn. You will then learn high-level learning skills such as speed reading, active listening, and note-taking. In the latter sections of the book, we will look at more specific accelerated learning methods that will help you learn a language, memorize lengthy number sequences, and remember names and faces. Turn the page to learn how and why you need to begin by setting yourself up for success.

Your Free Mindfulness E-book

I really appreciate the fact that you took an interest in my work!

I also think it's great you are into self-development and proactively making your life better.

Therefore, I would love to offer you a free, complimentary 120-page e-book.

It's about Mindfulness-Based Stress and Anxiety Management Techniques.

It will provide you with a solid foundation to kick-start your self-development success and help you become much more relaxed, while at the same time, becoming a more focused and effective person. All explained in plain English, it's a useful free supplement to this book.

To download your e-book, please visit:

http://www.tinyurl.com/mindfulnessgift

Enjoy!
Thanks again for being my reader! It means a lot to me!

Chapter 2: Setting Yourself Up For Success: How Your Attitude & Lifestyle Affect Your Learning

There are three components you need to put in place when becoming a star learner. One is a set of tried-and-tested techniques, which are featured throughout this book. The other pillars of success are a constructive mental attitude, and a healthy lifestyle. In this chapter, we are going to address the most important psychological and physiological factors that will shape your learning and, ultimately, your success.

First of all, consider how far you believe in your own ability to grow and change. Do you believe that, with the right techniques and guidance, you have the power to shape the way you live and work? Or do you fear that you will get everything wrong, and feel that your self-worth depends on your successes and failures? If this sounds familiar, you have what psychologists and self-development experts refer to as a "fixed mindset."[2] You are probably reluctant to venture outside your comfort zone. You are likely to hate receiving criticism, even if it is delivered in a constructive manner. This approach to life is not conducive to learning, because it lowers your expectations before you even begin. It will also render you afraid to push yourself, because you will be too scared of negative feedback.

A growth mindset is a much more productive foundation for anyone looking to learn a new skill. People with a growth mindset operate from the assumption that they can acquire whatever skills, knowledge, and even personal qualities they want. A growth mindset is not based on naïve optimism. It is built on a positive view of human nature, and this is a great basis for self-development and learning. If you believe that you can improve your skills and knowledge through your own efforts, you are more likely to put in the work necessary to achieve your goals. Focusing on growth means focusing on developing mastery and competence.

Those with growth mindsets may not enjoy receiving negative feedback, but they acknowledge that it can be very useful when moving forward. Perhaps most importantly, they do not interpret criticism as a threat to their overall self-evaluation. They see it as a necessary step on the road to success.

---

[2] Popova, M. (2014). *Fixed vs. Growth: The Two Basic Mindsets That Shape Our Lives.* https://www.brainpickings.org/2014/01/29/carol-dweck-mindset/

So how can you move from a fixed mindset to a growth mindset? The first step is to challenge your underlying beliefs about intelligence and ability. Research with children has demonstrated that when people believe their performance is down to innate intelligence and levels of ability, they are more likely to give up in the face of obstacles. After all, if you think that your abilities operate at a fixed level, there is little point in trying to compensate for your deficiencies. **However, children who are told that hard work is vital to success will develop a more positive attitude towards difficult tasks than those who are told that success is down to intelligence.** They are also more likely to enjoy better academic performance.[3]

Research into growth versus fixed mindsets has also revealed a counterintuitive phenomenon. Most people think that telling children that they are smart or talented whenever they get good grades will increase their self-esteem and motivation. In fact, the opposite is true! Well-meaning parents may tell their children that academic success means that they are smart, but this sets a child up to feel vulnerable and stupid when they come up against future challenges. Since almost everyone finds some tasks easier than others, the child is bound to feel bad about themselves sooner or later.[4]

What does this research mean for you? Essentially, you need to revise your beliefs about the links between achievement, intelligence, and effort. The single most important step you can take in setting yourself up for effective learning is to realize that when you believe **your efforts will take you further than your innate ability**, you will start to get the results you seek. The better your ability to persist when tackling a complex task, the better the final outcome will be. **You will want to keep going even when a task is challenging, because you know that with enough time and effort, you will prevail.**

You also need to realize that those who have achieved the most in life tend to have worked the hardest. Yes, some people are born with strengths in one or more areas, **but no genius or high achiever got to the top without some serious effort along the way.** Most also have growth mindsets that enable them to look failure in the face and carry on regardless. If you don't believe me, spend a few minutes researching a few of your idols. You will almost

---

[3] Ibid.
[4] Ibid.

certainly find that their work ethic and willingness to take on increasingly difficult challenges have been crucial to their success. Alternatively, ask your high-achieving friends or relatives how they got to where they are today. They won't tell you that the secret to success is to restrict your growth, limit your confidence, and take a passive approach to life!

Remembering your past efforts will also promote a growth mindset. Make a list of the skills you currently possess. Now make a note of the effort you needed to expend in order to acquire each ability. Assuming you have accumulated at least a few new skills since birth – and this includes reading, writing, and playing basic games – this exercise will prove that not only do you have the ability to expand and grow, but also that you need to put in effort if you want to change.

The second psychological aspect of learning is motivation. As I mentioned in the introduction to this book, most people assume that those who have achieved the most must have it in abundance. Most of us have been taught that hard work and hours of toil generate success, so this idea seems correct on an intuitive level. Fortunately for those of us who experience normal energy fluctuations, you do not need to rely on intrinsic motivation to see you through. No-one has limitless "get up and go." Thomas Frank, the creator of College Info Geek, points out that motivation will only get you so far. It is action that will determine the final result, not your level of motivation. However, feeling motivated does make the process of learning much more enjoyable, so it is worth developing the ability to increase your drive and initiative.

The truth about motivation is that it does not show up on command. **It must be cultivated.** Frank emphasizes that when someone complains that they can't get sufficiently motivated to tackle a task, the real issue is that they are reluctant to face up to the underlying problem. The underlying problem is that they aren't willing to try something new that could boost their motivation. This may seem like a subtle distinction, but it's important. After all, the implications are different in each case. If you work under the assumption that you simply cannot drum up sufficient motivation, and that without motivation you cannot hope to get the results you want, then you are bound to feel helpless.

However, if you see your lack of motivation as a problem that can be fixed by a change in attitude, you are more likely to address the issue and ultimately restore your momentum. When the urge to work towards a long-term outcome is stronger than the urge to do something more fun in the short-term, we become motivated to work on a task. If you lack the drive to learn some new material, start by reminding yourself of the rewards you will reap as a result of your efforts. The classic example is exam grades. If you want to succeed on a test and gain a particular grade, you will need to ensure that you learn the material. Therefore, the first factor to bear in mind when thinking about motivation is that your short-term urges and your long-term goals may act in opposition to one another, and that this is normal. Fortunately, you can keep them in balance by learning to ride out your unhelpful short-term urges whilst reminding yourself of your long-term goals.

Another thing to consider is the negative consequences of failing to put in the necessary work. These may range from feelings of disappointment when receiving a lower grade, to missing out on a job opportunity because you didn't learn enough about the company you want to work for prior to attending an interview. The more vividly you can imagine these consequences, the more likely it is that you will find the necessary motivation to work. Finally, the number of distractions in your environment will also determine how readily you will be able to commit your attention to one task. To maintain a suitable level of motivation, you need to devise ways of adjusting the above factors. Once you have established systems that work well for you, you will no longer have to hope that motivation will magically show up. You know that you have laid the groundwork, and you will be more likely to succeed.

The type of system you build will depend on your circumstances, your personality, and the type of task you are undertaking. For example, if you are primarily concerned with the rewards you could enjoy as the result of your work, adding more incentives may work well. Obviously, you will be working towards a key outcome, such as fluency in a new language, but you could also set up small rewards along the way. If distractions are holding you back, you can take a proactive approach by downloading an app that blocks you from particular sites for a predetermined length of time. You could also turn off your phone and place it in another room. If you give into temptation, you will at least have been forced to confront the fact that you are walking away from your work! **These systems require little motivation to maintain once they turn into habits.** If a particular app is always open when you log onto your computer, you are more likely to use it. **If you always leave your phone in a separate room during your study sessions, it will soon become second nature.**

What should you do if you cannot take the initiative to put these practical measures in place? It may be time to rethink your attitude. The harsh truth is that you need to take responsibility for making sure that your work gets done. No-one else can tell you how to set up a system that works for you, and no-one can force you to pay attention to the material you are trying to learn. Stop viewing yourself as a victim of circumstance, and start thinking about the opportunities that learning will afford you in the future. Taking responsibility for your own learning will make you feel empowered. You can be your own biggest obstacle, or your biggest cheerleader. It all comes down to your perspective.

Another approach is to examine your motives. Embark on some serious self-assessment. Get straight to the heart of the matter. Ask yourself why you are trying to learn something in the first place. Are you just trying to impress someone else, or perhaps train yourself for a new job that you don't really want? When you resist taking action, even when you think it will benefit you in the long run, it's time to dig deep and look at your original motives. Either find a good reason to continue with your current quest, or change your focus to something that fits with your interests and vision for the kind of life you want.

Along with a constructive attitude to learning, you also need to ensure that you are setting your body and brain up for success. A good diet and regular exercise are essential. Research with adults who were denied a well-balanced diet in childhood has shown that a poor diet is linked to below-average IQ and impaired cognition.[5]

Some foods are less brain-friendly than others. A high-sugar diet has a negative impact on learning abilities. Specifically, there is scientific evidence showing that foods and drinks high in fructose – a common form of sugar that is added to many processed products – limit the brain's ability to learn and recall information.[6] **Cut back on refined sugars and processed grains when you need to give your brain a boost.**

You may have heard the old saying, "Fish is good for the brain." It turns out that omega-3 fatty acids, which are found in oily fish such as mackerel, have a positive effect on memory and

---

[5] ScienceDaily. (2006). *Effects of Nutrition On Learning.* www.sciencedaily.com/releases/2006/07/060721203414.htm>
[6] UCLA Newsroom. (2012). *This is your brain on sugar: UCLA study shows high-fructose diet sabotages learning, memory.* http://newsroom.ucla.edu/releases/this-is-your-brain-on-sugar-ucla-233992

information retention. In fact, consumption of oily fish has been shown to lower the risk of Alzheimer's disease.[7] If you don't like fish or other natural sources of omega-3, such as nuts, you can buy it as a supplement in health stores.

A good sleeping pattern is also essential if you need your memory to function at its optimal level. If you are trying to learn a lot of information in a relatively short period of time, you may be tempted to cut back on sleep to squeeze in more study time. This will backfire, because we need between seven and nine hours of high-quality sleep if we are to maximize our ability to recall information the next day.[8] Rather than last-minute cramming, you need to improve your time management skills, implement solid learning techniques, and get into the habit of going to bed and rising at the same time every day.

Finally, exercise is also a powerful tool to have in your learning arsenal. Physiologists and psychologists have discovered that regular moderate exercise helps safeguard the structure and function of brain cells, which in turn boosts cognitive function.[9] This includes memory! You don't need to spend hours in the gym every day. Working out three or four times a week is enough to reap the benefits of physical fitness.

As you can see, the way in which we think about learning can make a significant difference. A few simple lifestyle adjustments will also create a solid foundation for success. With a positive mental attitude in place, you can begin to implement practical techniques that will allow you to absorb information quickly. In the next chapter, we'll look at a method that will help you assimilate ideas at a rapid rate.

---

[7] Morris, M.C., Evans, D.A., & Bienias, J.L. (2003). Consumption of Fish and n-3 Fatty Acids and Risk of Incident Alzheimer Disease. *Archives of Neurology, 60, 7,* 940-946.
[8] Gais, S., Lucas, B., & Born, J. (2006). Sleep after learning aids memory recall. *Learning & Memory, 13,* 259-262.
[9] Meeusen, R. (2014). Exercise, Nutrition and the Brain. *Sports Medicine, 44, 1,* 47-56.

Chapter 3. How To Absorb Information Rapidly: Learning To Read More Quickly Than You Ever Thought Possible

Even in this digital era, much of the information we seek out comes from books and magazines. When you decide to expand your knowledge on a topic, you may watch YouTube videos and read online summaries, but most people still buy books on subjects that most interest them. In this chapter, you will discover how to get the most from your reading time. You will learn how to boost your reading speed, how to pick out the key points of any book or article, and why you should always be reading multiple books at the same time.

Speed reading is perhaps the ultimate skill that you should acquire if you want to improve your learning ability. The faster you can absorb information, the more efficient a learner you will become. The average reading speed of a US adult is 300 words per minute.[10] The average nonfiction book is between 50,000 and 75,000 words in length. This means that it will take most people around three and a half hours to read a 60,000-word book. If you have plenty of time to devote to reading, this isn't a problem. Unfortunately, most of us do not have much free time during the average week. This is why speed reading is such a great tool!

Tim Ferriss, widely renowned for his work in the field of productivity and self-development, believes that speed reading can increase reading speed by over 300%.[11]
The first step is to assess your baseline reading speed. Find a new book that you haven't read, and open it to a random page. Using a timer, find out how long it takes you to read a single page. Calculate the number of words on the page by multiplying the number of words on a single line by the total number of lines. If you want to be really precise, you could count every word on the page individually, but an estimate is good enough for the purposes of this exercise.

The next step is to understand how long your eyes fixate on printed words. In other words, how long do you allow your eyes to linger on a word or line? The longer your fixation time, the slower your reading speed. You need to train your eyes to move along a line of text in a smooth motion. To do this, position a pen beneath the first word on a page, and then move it underneath the

---

[10] Ferriss, T. (2009). *Scientific Speed Reading: How to Read 300% Faster in 20 Minutes.* https://tim.blog/2009/07/30/speed-reading-and-accelerated-learning/
[11] Ibid.

words as you read. Your eyes will slide across the page, and your reading speed will increase. At this point, you do not need to worry about whether you are actually understanding the words you are reading. The point of the exercise is to train your visual reflexes.

Next, you need to train your peripheral vision. Most people look at the margins of each page when they read a book. **This is a waste of time.** Train your eyes to hone in on the first letter of a line, before immediately moving to the next once they have read the final word. To train yourself to read in a more efficient manner, place the tip of a pen underneath the second word of a line. When you reach the penultimate word, move the pen to the line below. This trains your eyes to focus on the words, rather than on the space around them.

Once you feel comfortable reading in this way, begin with the third word on each line. This may feel strange at first, but within a few minutes you will be accustomed to reading in this manner. You should soon be able to read at a speed of two lines per second. You do not need to concern yourself with your comprehension. At this stage, you are still training your reflexes. After a couple of practice sessions, review your reading speed. It should have increased by a significant amount! Continue to use the pen as a tracking aid for a few more sessions until your new reading style becomes second nature.

Two bad habits you should watch out for are mouthing and regression. If you tend to move your lips whilst reading a piece of text, you will cause your reading speed to slow down. Our eyes work much faster than our mouths, so you need to eliminate this behavior if you want to read more quickly. Fortunately, the drills outlined above will help you achieve this goal, because your mouth will not be able to keep up with your eyes! Regression is another unhelpful habit that these exercises will eliminate. When you regress during reading, your eyes go backwards, meaning that you reread words or lines. Some people even jump backwards several lines or by a couple of paragraphs, especially if they are worried that they have somehow overlooked some important details. This can be remedied by training yourself to read each line quickly, using the pen exercise given above. Once you know that your reading skills have improved, you will not worry that you have missed a key point.

Once you have increased your reading speed, you need to make sure that you are still able to understand what you have read. When you have finished reading a section, pause and ask yourself if you have understood the key message contained within the text. If you cannot summarize the text, read it again. Your aim here is to increase your reading speed whilst still being able to understand the words on the page. This comes with practice, so commit yourself to speed reading for at least half an hour each day.

Before you read a piece of text, you should familiarize yourself with the context of the work, and think about the main subjects the author will address. This background knowledge will help your brain makes sense of the information, even if you don't take in every single word. If you are reading a textbook, look through the review questions at the end of a chapter before approaching the core content. This will clue you in on the key points the author has included. You also need to make sure that you will be able to read without background noise or other distractions. A library or other quiet setting is perfect for speed reading.

The best long-term method of improving your reading skills is to broaden your vocabulary and general knowledge. This isn't a strategy that you can implement within hours or days, but it is one of the best ways to develop outstanding reading skills. Read widely, and read books and magazines from a number of genres. When your general knowledge improves, you will not need to spend precious seconds trying to understand what a cultural reference may mean, and you won't have to interrupt your reading to look up the meaning of a word or phrase.

In an ideal world, we'd all be able to choose our own reading material. Unfortunately, we sometimes have to read text that bores us. It's easy to find yourself drifting off into a daydream when you are trying to get through a heavy textbook. There are two key tips that can help you stay on track. The first is to take regular breaks. The human brain is incapable of concentrating on a topic for more than 50-90 minutes at a time. Take a 15-20 minute break every hour or so.[12] **Do not push yourself further in the hope that you will finish your reading more quickly, because even if you reach the end of your book sooner, your comprehension will suffer.**

The second tip is to choose your reading location with care. If you try to read heavy material in bed, or in a comfortable chair, you will soon find yourself dozing off! Pick somewhere new,

---

[12] Patel, N. (2014). *When, How, and How Often to Take a Break.* https://www.inc.com/neil-patel/when-how-and-how-often-to-take-a-break.html

preferably a place that is not conducive to sleeping. Do not aim to maintain a steady speed as you read. Sometimes you will need to identify the most important points in the text, and these will warrant focused attention. Not all sections are created equal. Get into the habit of looking at the first and last sentences of each paragraph. Some will contain key concepts that you must learn in order to develop your understanding of a topic, whereas others simply elaborate on these main points or further explain an author's opinion. Most nonfiction books are written in paragraphs that begin with a key fact or piece of advice, and then close with either a summary statement or a link to the next section. With practice, you will quickly be able to identify whether a paragraph can be skimmed. Untrained readers frequently overlook section headings and chapter titles. Don't do this – they are there for a reason. They are helpful in signposting the main points within a text, and prepare you to engage with specific topics.

The above techniques will help you increase your reading speed, but how many books should you be reading anyway? Conventional wisdom teaches us that it's best to read one book at a time, otherwise we will become overwhelmed and unable to give any of them the attention they deserve. However, there are valid arguments to be made in opposition to this approach. For example, self-development expert Tai Lopez points out that reading multiple books at the same time allows us to synergize ideas from two or more titles, and devise our own unique perspective on a topic. As a result, we will feel more engaged with the subject and develop a deeper understanding.

This approach works even if the books cover a variety of topics. Great thinkers often combine ideas and concepts from two or more disparate fields. Reading more than one book at a time can help you do this too. Choose three books on your chosen topic. Set aside as much time as you can afford each day to read. Now divide that time by three – this is the amount of time you will spend with each book. **Even if you only have 15 minutes available each day in which to read, you will make considerable progress in terms of knowledge and self-development within just a few weeks.** When combined with speed reading techniques, you will be able to read about, and process, new concepts at a faster rate than ever before.

To increase the likelihood that the material will be committed to your long-term memory, make reading a more active experience by forcing your mind to process information. If you are wondering whether this entails taking notes, you are on the right track. Note-taking is an essential step in moving from reading to memorization and deep-level learning. However, it is only useful if you go about it in the right way. In the next chapter, you will learn about the best and worst note-taking systems, and how you can summarize information in a way that accelerates your learning.

Chapter 4: How To Learn By Listening

Reading is probably the most common way of accessing new information, but many of us will attend lectures and talk to other people when we want to learn more about a subject. Whether you are a college student who needs to understand their professor, or a businessperson attending a networking event, you will benefit from acquiring excellent listening skills. Over the course of the average day, we will spend 45% of all our communication time listening.[13] The best students and employees are those who are willing and able to take on board what someone else is saying.

Before you attend a talk or scheduled discussion, do a little bit of research. Just as you should skim headings before diving into a textbook chapter, it's a good idea to gain an overview of the key concepts in advance of a lecture. For example, if you are attending a conference on current trends and innovations in your industry, you could look on the conference website and find a list of the speakers you would like to hear. Visiting their websites, reading their biographies, and skimming a few recent interviews they have given would be excellent preparation.

To get the most from a talk, you need to ensure that you are using active listening skills. Most of us are guilty of allowing our minds to wander, and this will hardly set you up to learn new information. If you sit through a lecture with one eye on the clock, thinking about your plans for the evening or your favorite TV show, you are wasting your time.

Everyone with a functioning auditory pathway can hear words, but not everyone processes their meaning. So what are the factors that prevent us from making the most of a lecture? Part of the answer lies with social psychology. Active listening begins with an open mind. Obviously, when you go to a talk or listen to someone else speak in conversation, you should be there with the intention of learning. Unfortunately, too many of us hold onto our personal theories and beliefs to the extent that we shut out anything that contradicts our views. Human beings are very good at defending their beliefs, and this makes us poor listeners. Worse, we are prone to operating according to our biases, and often use faulty thinking strategies when forming opinions.[14]

---

[13] Valdes, T. (2012). *Listen Up! Part I: Learning the Manly Skill of Paying Attention.* http://www.artofmanliness.com/2012/05/02/how-to-listen-effectively/
[14] DeMarzo, P.M., Vayanos, D., & Zwiebel, J. (2003). *Persuasion bias, social influence, and unidimensional opinions.* London: LSE Research Online.

If you want to use your critical thinking skills – and hopefully, you value critical thinking – **it's essential to listen without giving into knee-jerk reactions**. Practice listening to speakers that hold different views to your own. Watching a few videos online is a safe way to rehearse this skill, because you can always turn them off if you become too angry or upset. **However, over time, you will discover that the world will not end just because someone is putting forward a particular point of view.** This will train you in the art of keeping your emotions in check. Once you have mastered this skill, you will be able to appreciate someone else's opinions, and then judge them in a logical fashion.

When you put aside your emotions and assess the merits of a person's argument, you can move onto testing your memory and comprehension with a clear head. Whenever a speaker pauses, take advantage of the gap to mentally summarize their last point. Could you explain it in a few words? **Ask yourself whether you could bring someone who had arrived late up to speed.** If you can't, you need to listen more carefully. You may also need to examine your assumptions around listening, and what it signifies. Most of us have been taught, whether implicitly or explicitly, that to listen without arguing or countering every point is to communicate agreement. This simply isn't true. You can give someone a platform and listen to them, even for hours at a time, without having to agree with them. Do not be so proud that you don't give a speaker the chance to be heard.

On a related note, our preconceptions and tendency to stereotype others can cause us to assume that someone is a great speaker before they even open their mouth. This is because we tend to believe that someone who possesses one attractive quality must be competent in other areas.[15] In psychology, this is known as the Halo Effect. For example, we tend to assume that good-looking people are more interesting and knowledgeable than those who are plain. There is no logical reason to suppose this is true, but many of us are biased in this way.

I must admit that I've been guilty of this on occasion. I once went to a talk on diversity in the workplace, which was to be given by a woman in her late sixties. As I took my seat, I found myself thinking that the presentation was bound to be dull, and that the speaker had been

---

[15] Grcic, J. (2008). The halo effect fallacy. *Electronic Journal for Philosophy*, 1-6.

chosen only because she was from an underrepresented group. Imagine my surprise when she asked us to consider whether we would take her message more seriously had she been thirty years younger. I realized that she had a point, and since then, I have worked to challenge the assumptions I make about strangers. This has almost certainly made me a better and more receptive listener.

If the topic of a presentation is dull, make connections between the material and your personal life. Use your creativity to come up with at least three reasons why the information will be an asset to you at some point. If nothing else, you might be able to impress your friends and family during a game of Trivial Pursuit. Ideally, you'll be able to draw on your past experiences to make the information feel more relevant. For example, let's suppose that you are learning about the composition and strength of various building materials. This may not seem especially fascinating, but you could make it a little more interesting by thinking about what your current home is made of, and the kind of material you would use if you had the chance to create the house of your dreams.

Asking yourself questions whilst listening to a talk will also help you concentrate on what is being said. For example, if the speaker tells you that they are about to provide you with an overview of the greatest French artists of the 20th century, ask yourself who is likely to be included on that list. If a professor says that they will begin their lecture by outlining a model by which a business can engage their customers, think about the processes and stages that might make up such an approach.

There are six types of question you can ask yourself as you listen: What, Where, How, When, Who, and Why. Write them at the top of your notepad, and use each at least once during the session. Anticipating the speaker's next point will also keep you focused. Assuming that they are presenting information in a logical fashion, you should be able to make a pretty good guess as to what is coming next. If you get it right, you will also get to enjoy feeling pretty smart!

Finally, do not overlook nonverbal cues. A speaker may be relying on their words and visual aids, but their body language and tone of voice can provide you with clues as to what you really need to know, and what you can safely ignore. For example, if they become especially animated when talking about a particular theory, it's safe to assume that they think it is interesting, important, or both. You can also respond with a few non-verbal cues of your own. As a speaker, it is disheartening to look around the room and realize that some members of the audience aren't interested in what you have to say. Help them out by leaning forward, nodding slightly after every point, and taking notes. This can trigger a positive feedback cycle. **A speaker who feels appreciated is more likely to put in the necessary effort to make their lecture more engaging. This makes their audience more interested.**

Bear in mind that not all speakers understand how to put together a good presentation. If you are finding it hard to pick out the most important parts of a talk, it may not be your fault. In my college days, I had to sit through many sociology lectures that were both chaotic and dull. One of my professors was an acclaimed expert within her field, but had the tendency to wander aimlessly from topic to topic. Most of us would start yawning within half an hour. If you have the same problem, you'll have to take extra responsibility for your learning by working from books in addition to attending class. Is it fair that you have to put in the extra work? No, but then life isn't always fair! Reframe the situation as a chance to undertake some independent learning.

Listening is a key skill that underpins much of the learning we do throughout our lives. However, in order to process new concepts, you must be able to transfer what you have heard to paper. In the next chapter, I'll teach you how to take notes that will help you learn more rapidly than ever before.

Chapter 5: Organizing Information: How To Take Notes That Get Results

In the previous two chapters, I showed you how to take in information via reading and listening. The next skill you will need to use when learning about a topic is the art of efficient note-taking. In this chapter, you will learn why most people take notes that don't help them consolidate their knowledge. You will learn how to develop a note-taking system that works for you, and helps you grow your knowledge in any area you please.

So what are the most common mistakes people make? Perhaps the worst note-taking habit is the tendency to take notes for no other purpose than to get everything down on paper. There is no point in trying to write out everything you have read or heard. Why? First of all, it's an impossible task in most cases. Unless you have read a very simple piece of text, or heard a talk that was only a couple of minutes long, it is not feasible to replicate all the information you want to learn. Few people have this much time to waste!

Second, this style of note-taking does not require any active engagement with the material. Your notes are not just summaries of information – making them is, in itself, part of the learning process. Mindlessly copying out everything you have read in a book, or attempting to note down every single point a speaker makes, means that you miss out on the opportunity to think about new ideas and commit them to memory. Effective note-taking allows you to discern between the most important ideas – the high-level concepts contained within a topic – and details that are not crucial to your overall understanding. It lets you hone in what you really need to know. There are at least five main approaches to note-taking.[16]

The simplest is the outline method, which entails writing a brief description of each key subject area on a piece of paper, and then adding additional details beneath them. It's best to use a computer if you are using this system, because it allows you to return to each major bullet point and then add smaller bullets beneath it. You won't have to worry about running out of space, and you won't have to rewrite your notes when everything gets too messy. Your aim is to create a hierarchy of the major topics within the subject area, and preferably, to summarize them all on a single page. If you have to use a piece of paper, or just dislike typing, make sure that you

---
[16] Frank, T. (2014). How To Take Notes in Class: The 5 Best Methods. https://youtu.be/AffuwyJZTQQ

leave several blank lines between each major heading.

Another well-known strategy is the Cornell Method. Take a page and divide it into three sections. Draw a margin two inches in width down the left side of the page. Draw a horizontal line across the page, a few inches from the bottom. These three sections are your "Notes," "Cue/Questions," and "Summary" areas. When the speaker makes a point that seems relevant, or you come across an idea in the book you are reading, jot it down in the "Notes" section. You do not need to concern yourself with laying out these issues in any particular hierarchy. In order to speed up the process, use short phrases instead of full sentences, and use symbols and small diagrams where possible.

You should then make use of the "Cue/Questions" column to note down words and phrases that will help you revise the material later. This process forces you to engage with the notes you have just made, which is a major advantage if your natural tendency is to shove your notes in your bag and hope that they will still make sense at a later date. Finally, the bottom section of the page is for a summary of the key terms, questions and ideas you need to learn.

This was my favorite method in college. When my professor talked about various sociologists and their theories, I used the Notes section to jot down my thoughts, and as a space in which to rewrite the main points of the lecture in my own words. I would then write the names of the most important theorists in the Cue/Questions column. I would also write quick questions that forced me to engage with the material. So I would write, for example, "Talcott Parsons," but I would also scribble "How did TP describe society?" These cues and questions proved to be a good way of testing my knowledge later on.

A more recent approach to note-taking was invented by Scott Young, who managed to work his way through the entire MIT Computer Science program in a year.[17] He credits his success to his great note-taking skills. He calls his approach the Flow System. The principles behind this system are the complete opposite to those underpinning hierarchy-based methods. Young argues that instead of trying to capture every detail of a lecture or book chapter, students should learn to emphasize the most relevant information, create their own depiction or transcription

---

[17] Young, S.H. (n.d.) *Learning on Steroids: Flow-Based Notetaking.* https://www.scotthyoung.com/learnonsteroids/KJdf342RK-09898JKBDSTDFnkquikPP3-Jan/FlowBasedNotetaking.pdf

of the information presented, and make connections between ideas. The final result should be a unique document that captures the gist of the content in a way the student will understand. Young states that it should be possible to learn information at the time of presentation, rather than having to return to your notes later. Needless to say, this can save you a lot of time if it works for you.

To get started, experiment with incorporating arrows into your notes. This simple step is a good way of training yourself to literally draw links between concepts. Arrows also work well in conjunction with boxes, bubbles, and other shapes. **Within minutes, you will end up with multiple diagrams that will resemble flow charts – hence this method's name!** Young also recommends using small pictures or doodles to accompany the diagrams. These will keep you engaged, and make the content more memorable.

Originality is another key component when taking notes in this style. **Every time you make a note, ensure it is in your own words.** Copying or transcribing is not an efficient means of committing information to memory. You should also make links between the new ideas you are hearing or reading, and those within your existing knowledge base. **This helps your brain appreciate that this new information is relevant.** When something integrates with your preexisting understanding of the world, you are more likely to remember it later.

"Backlinking" is another useful technique. When a new idea reminds you of something you heard or read earlier, be sure to create a visual connection between the two.[18]
The advantages of this system are that it forces you to use your creativity and engage your brain as you learn, which will accelerate your learning. On the other hand, some topics may be too complex for you to summarize on paper in a single session. If you are attending a lecture, the speaker may move too quickly through the content, and you might struggle to keep up. In some cases, you may have to use textbooks or other learning materials to supplement your understanding. If you are attending a talk, use your phone to record the lecture. (Bear in mind that it is best to ask the speaker's permission first.)

Another popular approach to note-taking is the mind map system. **The logic behind this**

---

[18] Ibid.

concept is that we don't learn facts and concepts in isolation. Even the most obscure ideas you encounter will have links to your preexisting knowledge. Advocates of mind maps reason that when you want to learn an idea, you should highlight the ways in which it relates to other concepts. In this respect, it shares similarities with the Flow System.

Mind mapping can be done the old-fashioned way, on a large piece of paper, or via apps such as SimpleMind and Mindjet Maps. Either way, the core principles are the same. You begin by writing the name of the topic in the center of the page. For example, if you were learning about low-carbohydrate diets, you would write "Low-carb diets" in the middle. As you gathered more information, you would start to identify the most important points that come up regularly in discussions on the topic – the health benefits of a low-carb diet, how much weight people usually lose when they follow a low-carb diet, and so on. Each of these ideas would be a "branch," illustrated with a single line radiating from the center of the mind map.

You can then use smaller branches to go into more detail on each of these points. For example, the second set of branches radiating from "Health benefits" might include "Improved insulin resistance," "Decrease in sugar dependency," and "Increased energy." You could then develop the concepts further by adding the names and titles of studies that back up these assertions. To consolidate your learning, you might then challenge yourself to replicate the mind map on another piece of paper.

Finally, you can use what Thomas Frank refers to as the "Lazy man's method of taking notes."[19] This technique is possible only if you can gain access to a speaker's notes or presentation slides in advance of a lecture. All you have to do is print a copy and then make notes on the slides whilst the speaker is talking. The advantages of this system are that it is straightforward, and you are unlikely to miss any of the main points because you already have the skeleton of the lecture in front of you. However, it doesn't allow you to arrange the information in a way that works best for you. For example, you won't have additional space to make extra notes on topics that are of particular relevance or complexity. As a result, you might have to spend time after class writing up your notes again.

---

[19] Frank, T. (2014). How To Take Notes in Class: The 5 Best Methods. https://youtu.be/AffuwyJZTQQ

There is another killer weapon you can add to your note-taking arsenal, but it requires practice - shorthand. Shorthand systems allow you to write paper-based notes at high speed. Instead of spelling out each word in the usual style, you use simple symbols and pencil marks. There are well-established shorthand systems you can learn, such as the Pitman Method. These are highly effective, but shorthand skills take weeks (if not months) to develop. Most of us have neither the time nor the inclination to attend shorthand classes. However, you can devise your own system instead. **For example, you could come up with marks that represent common prefixes and suffixes. As long as your notes make sense to you, it doesn't matter whether your symbols are part of any official system.** You can combine your personal shorthand with any of the note-taking methods listed above.

Which method is best? Some people find that the Cornell style is best for note-taking during lectures, because it enables them to rapidly capture their thoughts on paper. However, this method requires that you spend time writing a summary of the information recorded in your Notes section, which may not be practical if you need to leave the building quickly after a lecture or talk.

Those who prefer to use a computer to create neat documents may prefer to construct hierarchical notes that can then be quickly adjusted with a few clicks. Every system has its strengths and weaknesses. Set aside a day or two to experiment with each. You might find that different systems work best in different situations. For example, the Flow System may suit your needs perfectly when you attend a lecture, but mind mapping (which you will read about in Chapter 14) might work best when you need to summarize a book chapter.

Note-taking may not be easy, but once you find a method that works for you, it can be fun! It's satisfying to look back at your notes and realize that you have developed a valuable skill whilst furthering your knowledge. Do not obsess too much about what your notes look like. All that matters is whether they help you to learn a concept – whether they look nice is of secondary concern. In the next chapter, you'll put your notes to the test by using a quick, simple technique that will highlight any gaps in your understanding.

Chapter 6: The Fastest Way To Test Your Knowledge: The Feynman Technique

In this chapter, you will learn a technique that has the power to change your life. If you take only one lesson from this book, it's this - you don't need to spend hours experimenting with learning techniques, because those who have gone before you have already figured out precisely what works.

In this chapter, you will discover how to master the Feynman Technique. **This method is a straightforward process by which you can quickly develop an in-depth understanding of even the most complicated theories and topics.** Physicist and Nobel Laureate Richard P. Feynman came up with this approach. Although his work required him to deal in complex, abstract topics on a daily basis, he was renowned as an excellent teacher who could communicate these ideas to his students with ease.

Feynman's notion was that you cannot claim to fully comprehend an idea until you can simplify it. Have you ever had to pause whilst in the middle of giving an answer to a question because you realized, halfway through, that you don't actually know much about the subject under discussion? It's embarrassing, isn't it? These awkward moments illustrate the first principle underlying this technique. It's quite simple – **if you cannot provide a clear overview of a phenomenon, then you don't really understand it.**

The second principle is that it is much easier to commit something to memory if you have to teach it to others. Have you ever met a teacher or college professor who told you they could teach their material in their sleep? This is because they have explained the concept so many times over, it is permanently embedded in their memory. Furthermore, because each student is different, the instructor may have been forced to come up with new ways of communicating an idea. This consolidates the teacher's learning still further. A key advantage of the Feynman technique is that you can use it at any stage of the learning process. It is just as effective for those who are beginning to grapple with a concept as it is for those who feel confident in their understanding, but would like to double-check their knowledge.

To get started with this method, take a piece of paper and note the name of the concept you are studying at the top. This title should be brief. Think of the short headings you might see in a textbook – that's the kind of length you need. The next step is to write a paragraph outlining the concept in plain English. Imagine you are talking or writing to someone who has never come across this concept before. Add in a couple of diagrams if necessary. Include some annotations if your drawings are not completely clear.

The next stage entails brutal self-assessment. Look back over what you have written. Does it make sense? Are there gaps in your knowledge? Pretend that you have been asked to mark your notes as though they were an assignment. Use a highlighter or make notes in the margins to indicate what you need to revise. Now get out your books or original notes and reread the areas that still trip you up. If you are still in the early stages of learning about a topic, make doubly sure that everything you have written is completely correct. This may take a while, but it is an excellent way of consolidating knowledge you already have, and establishing where you need to put in some extra effort.

Finally, return to your explanation and make the necessary amendments so that it really is a simple, effective overview of the topic. Make sure that you haven't used technical terms or jargon as a substitute for a nuanced, in-depth explanation. For example, if you are trying to prepare for a test on thinking and learning styles, you may have fallen back on vague terms like "cognitive processing." **Ask yourself whether you really understand what such a term means, and undertake more reading around the subject to fill any gaps in your understanding**. Once you have closed the book or paused the video, can you write down a comprehensive description of the term or a detailed definition of the concept? **If not, repeat the steps above until you feel confident.**

Although the technique is simple, it requires a healthy dose of self-discipline. Why? Because it's easy to persuade yourself that you know more than you do, and that your explanations are clear. If you try and fool yourself, you will be wasting your time. Approach this exercise with a positive attitude. Do not frame it as a way of highlighting your areas of ignorance, but as a means of understanding how you can improve. I know it can be a little depressing if you have to write and rewrite your explanation a few times, but think about it this way – within half an hour, your comprehension will have dramatically improved. The Feynman Method is an incredibly efficient study tool.

If you want to add another dimension to this technique, don't just create a written explanation – go one step further and teach it to someone else in person. Find two people who are willing to work with you. The first should be someone who has no prior knowledge of the concept you are looking to explain. This will force you to break down the ideas into layman's terms. Ask them to be honest with you. If they find your explanations confusing or incomplete, they need to speak up. For this reason, it's best to choose someone assertive.

The second person should be someone who already has an understanding of the concept, and will be able to correct you if you go wrong. For example, if you are in college, this could be a student in your class who has succeeded in mastering the topic. They can not only tell you whether the language you are using is sufficiently easy to understand, but they can also serve as a fact check. After all, there is little point in remembering something if your understanding is incorrect in the first place! If you don't enjoy making written notes, use another medium instead. **For example, you could record yourself explaining a concept, and then play it back to identify any weak areas.**

The Feynman Technique is a great example of "active learning." In recent years, education professionals have come to realize that when students are guided to work out concepts for themselves, they are likely to retain their new knowledge. Traditionally, Western-style education has been teacher-centered. In all likelihood, if you attended regular school or college, you will associate "education" with the experience of sitting in a classroom, being forced to listen to a teacher or professor talk without interruption for an hour or two at a time. Sometimes, if a teacher is particularly engaging, this can be an effective and enjoyable experience. I had a chemistry teacher who would demonstrate chemical reactions on a podium, and everyone in the class usually found his lectures stimulating. However, I can't help but think that had we been given the chance to try the reactions out for ourselves, we would have retained the information to an even greater extent.

Another tip is to make use of analogies, because these can illustrate concepts in a way that make them come alive. For example, the human digestive system can be compared to a waste recycling plant, with the various organs and digestive processes all forming their own function when it comes to processing various nutrients.
If you are in college, you can apply these principles during class time. For example, if you are

not sure whether your understanding of a concept is correct, you could raise your hand, quickly outline what you believe your professor is saying (using your own words), and finish with "So have I understood you correctly?" If you have, then you will have consolidated your own learning, which is a great result. If you haven't managed to take in what you have been told, then your professor will have the opportunity to correct you, which is also an excellent outcome! Of course, if the topic under discussion is particularly complicated, it's best to talk to the professor outside of class or via email. Otherwise, you risk taking up too much class time, which will not make you very popular! Sending and receiving email will also provide you with a written record that can help you review information at a later date.

If you are given the chance to provide feedback on a class that is traditional and "teacher-centered," take the opportunity to encourage the class leader to employ more active learning strategies. Suggest on any forms you are invited to fill out that students be asked to work in groups, undertaking exercises that require them to take turns explaining the concepts to one another. You could also put this idea into practice immediately if you are part of a study group. Study groups have their advantages and disadvantages – we'll return to this topic later in the book – but they offer you a valuable opportunity to discover how much (or little) you understand within a few minutes. **For example, sitting in a circle and taking turns to explain a complex theory can help everyone engage with the material and identify areas of strength and weakness.**

The Feynman Technique can put you on the right track and allows you to test your knowledge, but it is just one of many techniques that fall under the broader umbrella of experiential learning. In the next chapter, you'll learn more about this approach, and how it can help you learn new information at a rapid rate.

Chapter 7: Learning By Experience & Reflection: Experiential Learning

Your most vivid memories probably aren't of the textbook pages you've read, or the equations an instructor once drew on a board during class. Instead, your strongest recollections are likely to be your personal experiences. Your memory is not like a camera or camcorder – we do not and cannot remember everything with the same degree of accuracy, even when we want to! It's unlikely that you will be able to remember the exact words and images on a presentation slide or handout. It's more probable that you will remember how you felt during a particular class (e.g. "It was so boring!") or any incidents that gave you key feedback on the progress you were making (e.g., when you failed a test). **Feedback that inspires emotion and even inspiration pushes us to learn more quickly and efficiently.** In this chapter, you will discover why "learning by doing" is the most effective way of developing a new skill, and how you can begin to put this approach into practice.

Before we dive into the steps you'll need to take, I want to outline the theory behind experiential learning. The organizational psychologist David Kolb put forward a model known as the Kolb Experiential Learning Model.[20] Kolb was interested in how people learn, both in business and in education. His key insight was that experience really is the best teacher. He built upon this idea by outlining how, exactly, it might work in practice. His model includes four stages: Experiencing, Reflecting, Generalizing, and Applying. This model can be used to explain how we learn, both within and beyond formal education.

To get the most from this model, you need to understand precisely what it is that you need to learn. This might sound obvious, but in order to make the best use of your time, you should set specific goals. For example, if you need to learn how to use the simple past tense for French class, make sure you are clear on what, exactly, this entails. Do you need to learn it in the context of conversation, in the context of written language, or both? Know your goals, and write them down if possible. Doing so will allow you to ask yourself, "Is this activity moving me further towards my goal?" If at any point the answer is "No," you'll be able to get back on track within seconds.

---

[20] Kolb, D.A. (2015). Experiential Learning: Experience as the Source of Learning and Development. Upper Saddle River, NJ: Pearson Education.

To apply the first step in the model, you need to get yourself in a position to accumulate experience. Ask yourself when and how people use the skill you want to acquire, or implement the knowledge you are hoping to develop. Continuing with the instance above, you may reason that people who are using the simple past tense in French are likely to be French speakers who are having conversations with one another. Where might you be able to interact with such people? One means of accessing this kind of experience is to download and use a language app that connects you with people who speak French, such as HelloTalk. Within minutes, you could then find a French speaker who will be willing to talk about past events with you and correct any mistakes you are making.

I love these kind of apps, because you get to speak to a real live human being. This makes the process of learning a language a lot more engaging. Compare the experience of live conversation with the dull vocabulary exercises you tend to see in textbooks, and you'll see what I mean. I currently talk with two native Spanish speakers every week. It's a perfect arrangement – we both want to learn each other's languages. We are all busy people, but just ten or twenty minutes of small talk is enough time to practice common vocabulary and tenses. I get immediate feedback, and I learn at a much faster rate than when I try and increase my knowledge of Spanish using books.

In addition, there is also an element of peer pressure, which is no bad thing. I feel compelled to make a real effort, because I know they are doing the same, and I want to learn their language at least as well as they are learning my own! Another bonus is that I get to practice listening to native speakers and becoming accustomed to their accents, which will serve me well when I next go to Spain. I've also started listening to podcasts in Spanish, and watching Spanish films – naturally immersing yourself in the language is a great way to speed up your learning. You could even play radio shows or audiobooks whilst doing chores. As you gain a better grasp of the language, you can start to read books written by native speakers.

To use another example, let's say that you are taking a course in nutrition and public health, and need to develop an understanding of how food labels can be used to help people make better food choices. You may also have to learn about the standard recommended intakes for adults and children. Your goals would therefore be to memorize the key figures regarding recommended nutritional intake, and to be able to explain, using at least five distinct points or arguments, the ways in which food labeling can be used in the maintenance of a proper diet. How could you use experiential learning in this case? Think about the ways in which people actually use food and prepare dishes. They go to the store, pick out ingredients, take them home, and put together a recipe. If they are health-conscious, they will pay attention to the nutritional information on the packages, and come to learn what kinds of foods will help and hinder them in their quest to make better choices.

You could do the same. After looking up a few recipes online and checking out their nutritional profile, you could then experiment with new ingredients and meals for a couple of weeks. You would not only learn a lot about how ingredients can be combined to make a healthy dish, but you would also get to try some new foods. Sitting down and working out how each food could fit into a balanced meal plan would force you to engage with the subject, and would also help you understand how your new knowledge is relevant to everyday life. When it came to sitting for your nutrition exam, I'd be willing to bet that you'd be in a better position to remember the basics of nutrition than if you had just tried to memorize a chapter in a textbook.

Once you have accumulated some valuable experience, you need to take a step back and make a conscious decision to think about what you have learned. You are now at the "Reflection" stage. At this point, using the Feynman Technique to summarize your new knowledge would be a great idea. Next, go one step further and consider how far this learning style has helped you. Was it engaging, did it make the topic come alive, and was it an efficient use of your time?

Hopefully, you should be able to answer "Yes!" to all these questions. If not, what might you do differently next time? **Ask yourself whether your activities have moved you closer to your goal and, if not, how you could adjust your approach in the future.** Once you have developed the ability to think about the process of accumulating new knowledge, you will start to understand why experiential learning is considered a skill in its own right, not just a means of absorbing a particular set of facts or mastering a specific practice. Did you know that musicians, who typically have to learn via direct experience of playing an instrument, enjoy a distinct advantage when it comes to learning about other topics? Research has shown that they not only tend to score better than non-musicians on tests of music-related skills, but they also tend to learn other types of information at a more rapid rate.[21]

Why is this? When someone learns how to play a musical instrument, they are training themselves to pay attention to several types of stimuli at once – their sense of touch, their sense of sight, and their sense of hearing are all harnessed at once. This improves a person's overall cognitive ability and ability to pay attention.

In addition, the feedback a musician gains from practicing their instrument is instantaneous. For example, a saxophonist who plays the wrong note will realize immediately that they need to change what they are doing. **Experiential feedback teaches you that experience is the best teacher, so it encourages you to become comfortable with failure and to embrace feedback as a springboard to success.**

Experiential learning also teaches you transferable skills that will benefit you in every area of life. You will not only learn a skill or theory required for a test or specific project, but you also learn how to learn! For example, if you master the art of reflecting on your experiences and adjusting your approach on your next attempt, you will be an asset to any workplace, because you will always take responsibility for your own outcomes and be willing to face your weaknesses. Experiential learning also teaches you that your contributions are valid and worthwhile, which improves your confidence and capacity to work with other people. If you have children, you can encourage them to master everyday skills by trying, failing, and using feedback to move themselves one step closer to mastery. Needless to say, if you are in a teaching or mentoring position, you should do all you can to encourage your students or trainees to learn through experience. You don't have to use the phrase "experiential learning" – "learning by doing," "trial by fire," and "being thrown in at the deep end" are all perfect ways of summarizing this approach!

Once you have reflected on the learning experience, you can start to generalize what you have learned, and then apply it. For example, once you have mastered a few recipes, you can then start applying the skills you have learned (mixing, accurate measuring, and so on) to other culinary experiments. You will start to appreciate how your skills can be generalized, and how

---

[21] Sprouts. (2015). *Experiential Learning.* https://youtu.be/aF63HHVbpQ8

they can benefit you in other situations. For example, you might learn that thorough mixing is essential to baking the perfect cake. You would then form a generalized rule – "When baking, you should always take the time to mix the ingredients until even the smallest lumps have gone." In the future, you would then apply this rule when making other baked goods such as cookies. By testing the cookies, you would obtain further feedback and test whether your general rule is correct.

You will have noticed by this point that the Kolb model can best be thought of as a cycle. Conventionally, those who try to learn using this model begin with experience. However, there is no reason why you can't begin elsewhere in the cycle. For example, you might have come up with your own generalization, apply it, gain some valuable experience, reflect on what worked, and so on.

Or you might start by undertaking some reflection, devising a few ideas that could potentially work, then coming up with some rules and testing them out. However, Kolb was firm on one point – deep learning can only really occur when someone moves through all of the stages.[22]

Experiential learning is a fantastic way of developing your knowledge, especially if you are learning a practical skill. The principles outlined in this chapter will help you accelerate your learning, whether you want to become a great pianist or understand how to conjugate verbs. However, sometimes you will need to use a specific experiential technique that is tailored to an academic setting. In the next chapter, I'll show you a deceptively simple technique that allows otherwise average students to achieve superstar status within just a couple of weeks.

---

[22] McLeod, S. (2013). *Kolb – Learning Styles*. simplypsychology.org

Chapter 8: The Killer Strategy That Separates The Best Students From The Rest Of The Class

When asked what factors make someone a superstar student, most people say that it all comes down to IQ, that it's likely to be the result of "hard work," or a combination of both.[23] This is a pretty intuitive answer. As you already know, some people are smarter than others. We also know that nothing worth having in life is achieved without some degree of hard work. So the theory that the people who secure the highest grades must be naturally clever, and also inclined to put in long study days when required, seems to hold up.

However, research suggests that IQ isn't actually a powerful predictor of a student's grades. Furthermore, the number of hours they devote to studying doesn't correlate with their marks. So what is the magic ingredient? In brief, it's all about their willingness to undertake a very specific form of experiential learning.[24] **In this chapter, you will learn how to apply experiential learning theory to the most feared form of assessment among college students – exams – using one underrated but highly effective technique.**

If your college days are long gone, you may be tempted to skip this chapter. Following graduation, most people never want to think about exams again! This is completely understandable if you have experienced exam-related trauma. Too many of us have almost been reduced to tears by exam pressure, or had our minds go blank in the middle of a test. I failed a history exam during freshman year for this very reason. I had spent hours reading and rereading about the role Russia played in World War II, but as I sat down to write my first answer, it all just seemed to evaporate from my mind.

What if you learned how to handle exams with ease? What if tests – any kind of test, not just exams – inspired excitement instead of fear? You might feel confident enough to retrain for a more inspiring career, take a scuba diving test, or start a martial art and begin working towards your first grading. I'd encourage you to read through this chapter, and learn from its key principles, whatever your age or life stage.

---

[23] Barton, D. (2015). *What do top students do differently?* https://youtu.be/Na8m4GPqA3o
[24] Ibid.

So what is the magic technique so beloved of the highest performers? Douglas Barton, founder of Elevate Education, has undertaken extensive research with high school students around the world. He and his team have found that the more practice examinations an individual undertakes, the higher their grades. There are other factors that dictate academic success, but the key predictor is the number of hours spent rehearsing the exact type of exam they will have to undertake in order to earn their grades.

This doesn't mean that students shouldn't make notes, attend lectures, read widely around the topic, or neglect to use any of the key study skills that can help them excel. However, the results are indisputable – if you are serious about achieving outstanding grades, you are going to have to devote as much time as possible to getting hold of practice papers, and using them to hone your test-taking skills.

Students often make the mistake of using all their preparation time to learn factual material they believe will come up on the test. Their intentions are good, but this approach demonstrates a lack of appreciation regarding the actual nature and purpose of an exam. Yes, exams are a test of knowledge. At the same time, they are also a test of skill. You need to show that you have paid attention to the material covered in class, but also that you can apply this knowledge and communicate it in a format requested by an examiner.

Practicing exam papers is experiential learning at its finest. In taking a practice test, you are directly experiencing the process of taking the kind of exam you will have to sit. When you grade your own efforts, you are reflecting on what you have learned, and where you need to develop your knowledge. You can then tailor your study strategies to address your weak areas before trying more exam questions, marking your paper, and so on.

Most college professors and teachers know that practicing exam questions is a great revision strategy. You have probably heard them say something like, "You'd be well-advised to look over some papers," but most don't bother pushing this point home. Why? Because they know full well, as Douglas Barton's research has shown, that most students are not going to take their advice.

What if, for some reason, your instructor will not provide you with practice test papers, or you can only access one or two? You are going to have to get creative and compile your own questions. Look back over the course syllabus. Note down the style of exam you will be sitting, and the main points covered in your course. Devising your own questions can take an hour or two, but it isn't a waste of time. On the contrary, it is a learning experience in its own right. **By taking on the role of teacher or instructor, you are forcing yourself to summarize the content and pick out the most important points. This can guide your study.**

Once you have written your own test paper, send it to your instructor or a TA who helps out in class. Ask them whether your questions are in the right ballpark, and whether you have understood the format of the upcoming exam. As long as they tell you that you are heading in the right direction, you can then move onto the next stage. As an added bonus, your dedication and proactive approach will really impress your teacher or professor. Even if you don't quite get the grades you want (although you are almost certain to do well if you put in the hours), this will come in useful if you want them to act as an academic referee in the future. Professors are always keen to help and support a student who takes their studies seriously.

If you know another student who also realizes how important it is to practice taking exams, why not write two or three papers each, then give each other a set of copies? You'll have twice as many papers for no extra effort. You could also agree to grade each other's exams, and provide overall feedback as to the quality of your answers.

How you use the practice papers is up to you. I found that working through a paper before I started exam preparation was a constructive exercise, because it became pretty clear whether I truly knew a topic, or was just hoping that I could somehow get through an assessment. **In other words, I would start with the "experiencing" part of Kolb's learning cycle.** Once I had taken my first practice test, I would then devise tactics for boosting my mark next time around. On the other hand, you may want to start in the reflection phase. This might consist of thinking about what you already know about taking exams, and what you already know about the topic. You could then come up with a strategy that you think will help you do well in the assessment. Next, you would use these conclusions – ideas that Kolb would refer to as "generalizations" – to tackle the questions.

Either way, the take home message is that practicing a test will inform you of what you already know, and it will also teach you where your exam technique could use a little practice. For example, you may have a good understanding of a topic, but feel panicky when faced with a question that demands you write several pages summarizing and evaluating the key points. **The beauty of this exercise is that you will soon hone in on exactly where your problems lie. You can then track down the right kind of resources that will allow you to tackle the issue.**

For example, if you have trouble structuring answers that need to be written as essays, you can find online tutorials that teach you how to put together a great answer. If your school or college has a good study skills center, you can ask for help from a student advisor. You will already be in a strong position, because you know exactly how they could help you. You will be far better off than students who come in for help because they "struggle with exams, but don't know why." **This strategy isn't just helpful; it can save your academic career. Barton points out that bad study habits can become rapidly ingrained, and can lead to a "cycle of disengagement."**[25] If you fall into the habit of working hard in an unstructured manner, you will keep on getting disappointing grades. It will appear that no matter how hard you work, there is no way to "win." After a few semesters, even the most motivated student will start to feel discouraged. When you repeat a habit – whether good or bad – it becomes more likely that you will repeat it in the future. The sooner you fix your bad study habits, the better! In this case, if you aren't working on getting better, you are training yourself to get worse.

Of course, to get the most from this strategy, you need to recreate the exam conditions as far as reasonably possible. Clear your desk, and allow yourself only the materials you will be permitted to use on the day. Under no circumstances must you look at your notes until you grade your own paper. Turn off the TV, background music, and any other distractions. You won't be allowed your phone in the exam room, so turn that off too. **Your aim is to practice recalling and communicating information under a specific set of circumstances.** Don't do this in pajamas either – wear similar clothes to those you will actually wear on the day, right down to your shoes and socks! These details will send a clear signal to your brain that these periods of practice warrant your complete attention.

In short, you need self-discipline to do this exercise successfully. It takes real personal strength

---

[25] Ibid.

to force yourself to sit down for two or three hours and carry out a task that doesn't bring you much by way of enjoyment. In addition, we can only think about high-level concepts for a finite period of time before our brains need a rest! No one is superhuman. **Successful learners know that they need to find a balance between hard work and enjoying their breaks.** Unfortunately, most of us tend to find excuses to slack off, even when we know that we need to work hard. For obvious reasons, this slows down the learning process – if you are not actually engaging with the material, there is no way that you will learn it!

As you grade your own paper, make a list of your errors. You will come across two kinds of mistake. One category can be described as "Complete errors." When you make a complete error, you have either forgotten a piece of information entirely, or have become totally confused as to its meaning. The other most common form of error is a "Partial error." In this case, you will have understood the basics of a theory or concept, but are hazy when it comes to the finer details. **You will now have a comprehensive overview of your strongest and weakest areas of understanding.** These two lists are useful in their own right, as they help you prioritize your study time. However, they also serve as the basis for another scientifically-proven learning strategy. In the next chapter, I'll show you how to transform these lists into a powerful tool that will consolidate what you already know, and sharpen your knowledge in those areas that require it.

Chapter 9: How To Use Flashcards Effectively

Lots of students use flashcards when learning new material. The traditional method entails writing a question or prompt on one side of the card, and the answer on the reverse. The reasoning behind this is pretty sound. A flashcard is an active learning strategy, because it forces you to search your memory stores for the right answer. It's much more effective than passive reading. Therefore, as far as study strategies go, it's quite good.

Unfortunately, most students are not getting the most from their flashcards. In this chapter, I'll teach you how to get the most from this classic learning strategy. This technique is useful for those studying virtually any academic subject. A well-written set of flashcards can help you study in almost any location. This makes them a good tool for people with packed schedules. Carry them around with you and use them when you're waiting for a bus, making a dull train journey, or even during commercial breaks.

There are numerous apps and websites that enable users to make and share their flashcards online. These include Cram (cram.com) and Brainscape (Brainscape.com). In some instances, these can be useful. If you need to absorb a large amount of information within a short space of time, they can put you at an advantage.

However, I personally prefer to use old-fashioned index cards and pens. Drawing up your own cards by hand provides you with an opportunity to review the topic you are studying, and it forces you to distil it down into bite sized pieces. If you use other people's flashcards, you miss out on this stage of the learning process. **The preparation of the cards is in itself an active learning strategy!** Using a website or app also leaves you vulnerable to distraction. Flashcard websites contain hundreds of thousands of cards, and it's easy to start clicking around and exploring subjects that look interesting, but aren't actually relevant to the topic you are trying to study.

Flashcards are useful when you need to learn language vocabulary, key dates, and terminology. With a bit of imagination, you can also use them to test your knowledge of models that include a number of stages. For example, let's say you wanted to memorize the stages of Kolb's model of experiential learning from Chapter 7. This model has four stages: Experience, Reflection,

Generalization, and Application. Instead of writing "Explain Kolb's model?" on a flashcard, it would be better to write several cards that test your knowledge of the various stages. Writing four cards would be far preferable to a single card that asks you to outline the entire model. This is because using four distinct cards quickly helps you identify which parts of the model you do and do not understand.

Sticking to the "One card, one question" rule also protects you from illusions of competence. The human brain is excellent at recognizing stimuli that it has encountered on previous occasions. However, recall is significantly more difficult. If you allow your brain to get confused between recognition and recall, you start kidding yourself that you "know" more than is really the case.

An example will show you how this works in practice. Suppose you wanted to test your knowledge of the Kolb model outlined above. Let's say that on one side of a flashcard, you wrote, "What are the four stages in the Kolb model of learning?" On the reverse, you wrote, "Experience, Reflection, Generalization, and Application." If your response to the question was "Experience, Reflection, Generalization" and the reverse of the card told you that you had missed a stage, you might tell yourself that it doesn't matter, because you recognize the right answer, even if you cannot recall it. This is a dangerous line of thinking, because in these cases you don't really know a piece of information, you only recognize it. Sticking to single questions with single answers is the surest means of overcoming this problem. For example, a better question would be, "What is the stage following 'Experience' in the Kolb model?"

Study guru Thomas Frank emphasizes that it's important that you understand when flashcards are not appropriate.[26] If you are looking to gain an overview of how different concepts fit together, flashcards are unlikely to help you develop this kind of understanding. Neither are they especially useful when you are learning a hands-on skill. **They are best used when trying to learn highly specific facts, so are perfect if you are preparing for a multiple-choice test or need to brush up on the finer details of a topic.**

In other words, they are not a substitute for high-level study of a topic. For example, if you were

---

[26] Frank, T. (2016). How to Study Effectively with Flash Cards – College Info Geek. https://youtu.be/mzCEJVtEDoU

studying for a philosophy exam, it would not be a good idea to write questions that require complex answers. For example, "Outline the history of dualism?" or "Explain a fundamental weakness of the ontological argument?" are too in-depth for flashcards. Writing out the correct answer to these questions on the reverse of the card would be impossible. Even if you were able to summarize the main points, you risk falling into the trap of teaching yourself that the concept is much simpler than it is in reality. Of course, you could use them to test your knowledge of the years in which arguments were put forward, or the names of various theories.

Use both words and pictures on your cards, because this will make them more effective than cards that feature words alone. This is due to the "picture superiority effect," a psychological phenomenon that relates to the way our brains pay attention to incoming stimuli.[27] In short, we have evolved to take note of images, not words. Written language has been around for a relatively brief time within human history, whereas we have always had to respond to stimuli in our environment, or else we would have been attacked by other animals, or fallen victim to natural disasters. Take advantage of this human tendency by drawing images that have associations for you. **Use diagrams, cartoons, miniature flowcharts, or whatever else makes the information more memorable.** These associations do not have to make sense to anyone else but you. It doesn't matter whether you are an accomplished artist. As long as you understand the image and what it represents, it's good enough.

For example, suppose you want to draw up a series of flashcards that test your knowledge of classes of drugs. Specifically, you want to teach yourself that barbiturates are depressant drugs. On one side of the card you could write "What type of drug are barbiturates?" The other side could read "Depressants," and be accompanied by a picture of a sad cartoon bat, shedding a tear. The "ba" at the beginning of the word "barbiturates" sounds a little like "bat," and the image of a crying bat is memorable. You may be tempted to save time by sharing flashcards with friends, but their power lies partially in the unique associations you form. You probably wouldn't understand why a particular image works for a friend or classmate anyway. We all have our own ways of looking at the world and making sense of complex information. You might not want to make flashcards for the fun of it, but once you start thinking creatively, it can feel

---

[27] Ibid.

satisfying to have made you own special study deck. If you feel frustrated by your drawing abilities, you can always print out pictures or illustrations from the internet. However, this can set you up for procrastination. Do not become too hung up on making pretty flashcards. It's what you do with them that is far more important.

As you put your deck together, ensure that the questions it asks of you will be suitably demanding. Do not create a set of flashcards that are all of the same level of difficulty. Just because the format is simple, doesn't mean that the questions cannot be challenging. Start with writing out a few straightforward questions that already feel familiar, but then deliberately set out to create flashcards that probe the depths of your knowledge. Imagine that you are writing a study deck for someone you really don't like very much – that's how challenging they ought to be! You could also pretend that you are working in the role of a professor or even a professional quizmaster. Answering tough questions may not be much fun, but your future self will thank you when it comes to sitting the test or exam.

When you work through the deck, say the answers out loud before turning over the card to reveal the answer. Stating an answer aloud helps you commit to an idea, and makes it less likely that you will try to fool yourself. If you are working alone and answering the questions "in your head," it becomes easy to tell yourself that you nearly got a particular answer right, so you'll just move onto the next card. **If possible, ask someone else to test you.** This forces you to state your answer clearly, meaning that there is much less room for self-deception. Other people won't try to convince you that your answer is good enough if you make a mistake!

Most people like to write a question on one side of the flashcard, and then the answer on the other. They then study the questions, try to learn the answers, and then test themselves by running through the questions. This is a good strategy, but it's even better to study the answers too. Why? If you know the question that accompanies an answer, you can recall information from both angles.

For example, if you are studying French vocabulary, you may write "Poisson" on one side of a flashcard, and "Fish" on the other. If you were to study the card by reading "Poisson" and then asking yourself what it means in English, you are training yourself to recognize this word as "Fish." That's all well and good, but what if you are asked to translate "Fish" to its French equivalent in an exam? You would stand a better chance of answering this question successfully if you had forced your brain to translate the same word back and forth between languages.

This also applies to specialist terminology. For example, suppose you were studying for an exam in human anatomy, with a focus on the digestive system. In this instance, you would need to teach yourself, among other things, that the gastric rugae is a term used to describe the ridged folds that occur within the internal wall of the stomach. On one side of a flashcard you would write, "What is the gastric rugae?" On the other, you would write a brief description of it, as given above. When revising for a test, you should use each side as both a question and an answer. Many students fall into the trap of assuming that a test will only ask questions from one direction. Be prepared! Make sure you can put a name to a description, and that you can provide a comprehensive definition of a term.

A final tip I'd like to pass on is this – always make at least two copies of your flashcards. It's easy to leave them in the library, lose them behind your desk, or have them fall victim to a spilled cup of coffee. If you are preparing for a vital exam, you cannot afford the time needed recreate your cards all over again. The ten minutes it takes to create a backup copy is a good investment of your time.

If you follow the guidelines in this chapter, your flashcards will help you learn facts and figures quickly. However, working your way through the cards over and over again isn't enough to consolidate your learning. Did you know that it's not just what you write on your cards that matters – it's also how and when you use them that makes all the difference? In the next chapter, you'll discover how you can use the principle of spaced repetition to learn more efficiently than ever before.

Chapter 10: Spaced Repetition: How To Realize The Full Potential Of Flashcards

Now that you have a set of flashcards that work for you, how can you get the most from them? You already know the basics, but there is an advanced study technique that will accelerate your learning still further. In this chapter, I'll show you how to apply the principle of spaced repetition to your study sessions.

Most of us accept that repetition is key in learning. As a rule, the more often you do something, the more likely you are to remember it. The old cliché, "practice makes perfect," is a common saying, and with good reason. However, there isn't a linear relationship between the number of hours you spend trying to learn information, and the likelihood that you will recall it successfully at a later date. Instead of studying information continuously, you need to know when and how to take breaks if you want to maximize the chance of later recall. This means you can streamline your study time, making the most of the hours you have available. If you spread your learning time over days, weeks, or even months, you can get more learning bang for your buck.

All psychologists know about the spacing effect. **Essentially, this theory explains how and why we are more likely to learn new material if it is presented in short sessions over a relatively long period of time, rather than during one period of continuous exposure.** Also referred to as distributed practice, spaced repetition takes advantage of the way in which the human brain learns, and how it is structured. In the psychological literature, repeated exposure in a short space of time is referred to as "massed practice," whereas sessions that are spread out are known as "spaced practice."[28]

Spaced practice was discovered in the early days of psychological research. In the late 19th century, a German psychologist by the name of Hermann Ebbinghaus (1850-1909) embarked on a program of study into learning and forgetting. He challenged himself to learn short nonsense "words," such as WID. He would read these word lists a predetermined number of times. He would then test himself later on, at various time periods following original

---

[28] Kang, S.H.K. (2016). Spaced Repetition Promotes Efficient and Effective Learning: Policy Implications for Instruction. *Policy Insights from the Behavioral and Brain Sciences, 3, 1,* 12-19.

exposure.[29]

His first finding was that, over time, we forget information that is presented to us. He referred to this phenomenon as the "forgetting curve," because when he plotted the results on a graph, the data points produced a steep downwards curve. Ebbinghaus stated that some people had greater capacity for retention than others, but the overall trend was the same – unless we are reminded of information, we forget it quickly. Specifically, he found that most of us will have forgotten half of what we have learned within three weeks from the point of initial exposure. He also realized that more repetitions do not equate to better recall. **He discovered that reading a set of information a total of 38 times was just as effective as reading it 68 times, if the 38 repetitions were distributed over three days.**[30]

In short time periods, massed practice offers an advantage when it comes to recall. On the other hand, spaced practice promotes significantly more recall over the long haul. For example, in one classic study, a group of students were challenged to memorize the Athenian Oath, a military oath that was recited by young men in ancient Greece. This oath is several lines long and contains language not often used in day-to-day conversation, so it was a tough challenge. One group of students heard the oath six times on the same day, whereas another group heard it read three times on the first day, then three more times a few days later. Whilst the massed practice group showed better recall immediately following the experiment, the spaced practice group showed much greater retention of the material a few weeks later.[31]

So why exactly does spaced practice work so well? The most common explanation is that, when you repeat a piece of information, you are reminding yourself of a prior occurrence. This forces your brain to work hard and retrieve the information. In order for this effect to occur, you have to leave a gap between practice sessions. During this period, your brain lays down new neural pathways that strengthen these new memories. Massed practice means that you miss out on this opportunity, because you don't have time to forget the information. **It may seem counterintuitive, but it seems as though you need to forget things in order to**

---

[29] Syndeon Soft. (2012). *The forgetting curve.* flashcardlearner.com
[30] Revunote. (2017). *The Spacing Effect.* revunote.com
[31] Ibid.

increase your chance of recalling them at a later date![32]

The "Deficient processing" theory offers a slightly different explanation. It states that when you expose your brain to the same piece of information over and over again within a short period of time, it registers the stimulus on the first couple of occasions, but then "switches off" as it realizes that you aren't feeding it any new information. If you think about it, we routinely block out irrelevant information in our daily lives, including things we have already heard or seen. For example, if you notice the sound of a water fountain when walking through a park, you are unlikely to keep focusing on it once you've registered the source of the sound. Our brains have evolved to filter out redundant "noise," and this tendency can't be turned off at will! Your brain automatically assumes that repetitions, or "copies," of information are useless and can be ignored.[33] Therefore, it makes sense that massed practice can only take you so far. **You need to give your brain some time and space so that it can be stimulated by another practice session.**

Now let's apply these research findings to flashcards. Start by gathering a few small boxes. Label these boxes, "Daily," "Every other day," and "Every two days." On the first day, place all of your flashcards in the "Daily" box. Go through each card in turn. When you answer the question correctly, put it in the next box. Every day, use the labels on the boxes to manage your periods of spaced practice. If at any point you fail to answer the card correctly, you must move it back to the beginning, i.e. to the "Daily" pile. You will need to consider your unique situation when deciding on the labels for your boxes.

The suggestions above assume that you are studying for a fortnight in advance of an exam. If your assessment is further away, then you will need to tweak this system so that the sessions are more widely spaced. In summary, whilst cramming just before an exam may help you remember information, you need to pace yourself if you want to really understand the material. This means that you will need to put together a study timetable well in advance of your tests. This system allows for no self-delusion. It's a binary process – if you get the answer on the card wrong, it goes back to an earlier pile, no exceptions. It allows you to relax, knowing that you are

---

[32] Ibid.
[33] Ibid.

paying attention to the cards that you find to be the most challenging. **If you tend to delay tackling the hardest material during a study session, this system will ensure that you no longer give into temptation.**

If you prefer to study using apps instead, you can choose from several well-known apps that allow you to make your own flashcards, and then engage in spaced practice. One popular option is Anki (apps.ankiweb.net), which is available across all platforms. Once you have built your flashcards, the software will then present them to you on your screen. You then tap a button to rate how easy it was for you to remember the correct answer, and Anki uses an algorithm to calculate when you next need to review the card. Other apps that serve the same purpose include Eidetic (eideticapp.com), and Repetitions (repetitionsapp.com).

You can combine this technique with any other study method, such as flashcards or exam practice papers. However, researchers in this area have found that spaced repetition works best when it is combined with tests that gauge the extent to which a student has learned the material.[34] This means that employing practice exams or flashcard-based questions, rather than making or reading notes, is the best way of promoting long-term retention and recall when combined with spaced practice. However, there are also a number of slightly left-field "learning interventions" out there, which some people believe are highly effective in accelerating the learning process. In the next chapter, we're going to look at an increasingly popular method that purports to improve your focus and memory retention with no effort at all!

---

[34] Ibid.

Chapter 11: Music, Binaural Beats, & Learning

If you have ever used the internet to research the science of learning, you will have come across advertisements for binaural beats, and other recordings that supposedly help the listener improve their concentration and capacity to learn. But do these claims have any merit? Has science proven that specific types of sound can aid in the learning process? **In this chapter, we'll look at the rationale behind these products, and consider whether they have any part to play in aiding learning and recall.** If you have ever wondered whether regular music – for example, pop songs -can accelerate your learning, you'll be pleased to know that the answer will be revealed later in this section.

To begin with, let's consider binaural beats. A quick search online will turn up thousands of YouTube videos that apparently harness rhythm to focus the brain. So what are these "beats?" A binaural beat consists of two different tones, at two different pitches. Each tone is fed into one of the listener's ears. However, the brain processes this input in such a way that the listener perceives a steady rhythm. **In essence, these beats are actually an auditory illusion created by the brain.**

Those who attest to the power of binaural beats claim that they work by inducing measurable changes in the brain's physiology. Our brain is continually sending electrical signals between its neurons. Specific patterns of electrical activity are referred to as "brainwaves." If you were to place electrodes on someone's scalp and hook them up to an electroencephalogram (EEG machine), you would see that their brain's electrical output resembled waves. Physiologists and psychologists have discovered that not only do brainwaves come in a range of characteristic patterns, but that certain patterns are associated with different mental states. For example, "Delta waves" are slow waves that occur when an individual is in a state of deep sleep. Other patterns, including Alpha and Beta waves, occur at a much higher frequency and are seen in individuals who are awake and alert to stimuli in their environment.

In theory, it should be possible to induce a particular state of consciousness by manipulating the speed and frequency of a person's brainwaves. The first people to report on this phenomenon were Cambridge-based researchers Adrian and Matthews (1934). They used flashing lights to alter their participants' brainwaves.[35] They noticed that depending on the way in which they flashed these lights, an individual's Alpha waves could be made to occur at a lower or higher frequency. The researchers concluded that when the human brain comes into contact with an external stimulus, its frequency will change in such a way that it will match it. So if someone experiences a light flashing rapidly in front of their eyes, their brain will automatically increase the frequency of its brainwaves.

But what about auditory stimuli? In other words, can sound frequency have a tangible effect on a person's brainwaves? The concept of adjusting someone's brainwaves and cognitive state via sound is referred to as "auditory driving."[36] In 2008, two researchers from the University of York, England, carried out a review of 20 studies on the application of binaural beats in a range of contexts. **They concluded that such interventions might help people feel more relaxed and less stressed (and by extension, more focused).** The results of six studies included in the review demonstrated that binaural beats can influence cognitive measures, including attention. However, the studies were of inconsistent quality, and the authors of the paper suggested that more research was needed on the topic.[37] Furthermore, some of the research studies mentioned in the paper did not support the notion that binaural beats have any significant effect on mood or cognition.

Since this review was published, many more studies have been conducted. **Although we do not yet know precisely how the brain "syncs" with external stimuli, some research has yielded compelling evidence that high-frequency beats improve concentration and feelings of alertness, whereas lower-frequency beats induce sensations of calm and a relaxed mood.**[38] The success of any particular intervention depends on the beat frequency, and scientists are still trying to establish the exact frequency that will yield the best results in specific situations. For example, a study published in the *Journal of Neural Engineering* experimented with beats of 5 Hz, 10 Hz, and 15 Hz frequency. Only binaural beats presented at a frequency of 15 Hz had any noticeable positive effect on working memory

---

[35] Siever, D. (2006). Audio-Visual Entrainment: History and Physiological Mechanisms. mindalive.com
[36] Frank, T. (2016). Brain-Enhancing Music and Binaural Beats: Do They Work? https://youtu.be/6HZlNm33kwA
[37] Huang, T.L., & Charyton, C. (2008). A comprehensive review of the psychological effects of brainwave entertainment. Database of Abstracts of Reviews of Effects (DARE): Quality-assessed Reviews.
[38] Colzato, L.S., Barone, H., Sellaro, R., & Hommel, B. (2017). More attentional focusing through binaural beats: Evidence from the global-local task. Psychological Research, 81, 1, 271-277.

function.

So what can we conclude? As yet, there isn't enough research to prove or disprove the idea that binaural beats can make a significant difference to someone's concentration and, by extension, their ability to learn. However, given that there are many free videos and tracks available online, I would recommend that you try it for yourself to ascertain whether it works for you. Bear in mind that some people may find binaural beats to be effective on account of the placebo effect – that is, they believe that the beats will help them learn, and this becomes a self-fulfilling prophecy. **This doesn't mean that the results are any less valuable for those who like using these tools.**

For example, even if they don't work quite as advertised, they can still be a great tool for blocking out annoying background noise. If you've ever tried to write an essay with the sound of people talking in the background, you'll know how distracting ongoing, low-level noise can be. There are also tracks available that combine beats with ambient music, which can reduce feelings of boredom without distracting you from the task at hand.

Noisli (noisli.com) is a popular app that offers 16 different types of background sound. These range from natural noises, including the sound of running water, to more industrial sounds, such as trains running over tracks. You can create a personalized ambient mixture by increasing or decreasing these 16 sounds until you find a setup that works for you. To save your unique configuration, you will need to set up a free Noisli account. Once you've signed up, you can share your ambient mixes with others, and also take advantage of Noisli's other productivity tools – a timer, and a distraction-free word processor. Personally, I've found the coffee shop noise to be best when writing, possibly because the background chatter creates an illusion that there are other people in the room, which spurs me on to complete tasks at a faster rate. The app can also be used to generate white, pink, and brown noise.

Mynoise (mynoise.net) also offers a wide selection of ambient noises and soundscapes. There are dozens of readymade sounds available on this site. Set yourself a strict time limit for exploring its library, or you'll risk losing some of your precious study time!
What about listening to regular music? Is it a good study aid, or merely a hindrance? People seem to fall into two distinct camps when this question comes up – or at least they did when I

was in college. Several of my classmates swore that they learned more with their favorite music playing in the background, whereas others maintained that lyrics were far too distracting. Study guru Thomas Frank recognizes that everyone has their own preferences. He recommends playing high-intensity music when performing mundane tasks that require little conscious thought, such as data entry. This is because such music increases your energy levels, and builds your momentum. However, when he needs to engage in a more complex task such as understanding a chapter in a textbook, only silence or instrumental music works for him.[39]

Some of us can only study in near-silence. For the most part, I appreciate silence when trying to grapple with a new concept. However, as Thomas Frank has also noted, silence can drive you a little crazy. If you are not used to spending time in a quiet environment, your brain will begin to fixate on anything and everything it can hear. For example, the clock in your kitchen that doesn't usually bother you might start to seem unusually loud once you've been trying to study for a few minutes. If you can't stand silence but find lyrics or regular instrumental music too distracting, try white noise generators such as SimplyNoise (simplynoise.com).

Scientists have yet to reach a firm conclusion regarding the effect of music on concentration. This is because there are so many factors to consider, including the type of music, the age of the student, their studying habits, and their familiarity with the music.[40] For example, educational psychologists have discovered that students do not tend to play music with lyrics while studying unless they are writing or thinking. Perhaps more importantly, students are capable of realizing when music is interfering with their performance, and are willing to turn it off when necessary.[41]

Although psychologists have not reached any definitive verdict, they believe that when a student is required to use the parts of the brain responsible for interpreting music on other tasks, their performance will suffer. If your brain is trying to make sense of complex sounds, this will interfere with your ability to analyze complicated concepts, which is why most people find it hard to focus on new ideas if they can hear lyrics playing in the background.

---

[39] Frank, T. (2016). *Should You Listen to Music While Studying?* https://collegeinfogeek.com/should-you-study-with-music/
[40] Kotsopoulu, A., & Hallam, S. (2010). The perceived impact of playing music while studying: Age and cultural differences. *Educational Studies, 36, 4*, 431-440.
[41] Ibid.

Interestingly, there are cultural variations when it comes to music and studying. Greek students are especially likely to play music, and Japanese students the least. Those from the US and UK are somewhere in the middle. Pop is the most common choice, and classical music the least popular genre.[42]

A recent study published in the *Journal of Applied Research in Memory and Cognition* looked at how differences in working memory dictate the extent to which music affects someone's performance on academic tasks. The researchers asked a group of undergraduates to undertake reading comprehension and math-based tasks whilst either listening to music or working in silence. Once they had finished, the researchers measured their working memory – in other words, how good each student was at paying attention to, taking in, and manipulating information. **Two key findings emerged. First, music had a detrimental effect on performance. Second, students with the strongest working memory capacity achieved higher scores.** Their ability to process more information in a short space of time protected them from the effects of the music.[43]

So what should you take from this discussion? Basically, although there are some key rules that apply to most people when it comes to studying with music, everyone is an individual and needs to find what works for them. Research suggests that most of us should avoid music with lyrics when undertaking complex tasks, but this doesn't mean that some people won't find it helpful! It's more important that you are honest with yourself regarding the effect music has on your performance. If your concentration is suffering as a result of playing music, exert some self-discipline and turn it off. Because listening to music doesn't require any active effort or even any movement, it's easy to trick yourself into thinking that you aren't really distracted at all. Don't cheat yourself out of quality study time. Get to know how your brain functions, and be ready to experiment with new ways of working if necessary. In the next chapter, we'll look at distractions from another angle. You'll discover why your attention may wander when you try to study, and how you can stay focused, disciplined, and immune to procrastination.

---

[42] Ibid.
[43] Christopher, E.A., & Talley Shelton, J. (2017). Individual Differences in Working Memory Predict the Effect of Music on Student Performance. *Journal of Applied Research in Memory and Cognition, 6, 2*, 167-173.

Chapter 12: How To Beat Procrastination & Get Down To Work Fast

Many of us don't have a clue how we learn best, and it isn't until we hit upon techniques that work for us that we begin to fulfil our potential. However, I'd argue that it isn't a lack of knowledge that holds most people back from developing their skills and boosting their learning capacity. I believe that one of the biggest problems learners face is one that everyone comes up against from time to time. It can be hard to spot, difficult to overcome, and can ruin even the most promising of careers. The name of this problem? Procrastination. **Unless you master the art of getting on with your work even when you don't feel like it, no amount of accelerated learning techniques can help you.**

Trying to make progress by using the other techniques in this book while leaving your procrastination problem untreated is like trying to apply paint to an uneven wall. You need a good foundation and a solid base if you are to enjoy a great finish. After all, if you can't even sit down and concentrate, you aren't going to get very far! **In this chapter, I'll give you a set of tried and tested techniques that will supercharge your focus and condense the time it will take you to learn new information.** These principles apply to all learners, whatever they are looking to master.

Sometimes, the simplest remedies are the best. Before you start trying any special anti-procrastination techniques, make sure you know what you are actually trying to accomplish. If you aren't sure where you want to end up, or how you will know whether you have been successful, you will feel overwhelmed. You will be seriously reluctant to get started. In my first job, I almost missed a couple of deadlines on major projects because I took the "ostrich" approach. I'd imagine the task to be much harder than it was in reality. **On a couple of occasions, I almost kicked myself when I realized how much more progress I would have made had I just been brave enough to sit down and work out what actually needed to be done.** Too often, we dwell on worst-case scenarios and make ourselves anxious for no real reason at all.

Think of it like this – if you discover that the project or goal is more manageable than you thought or feared, you can get started right away, reassured that it is within your reach. For example, suppose you have to learn how to play a challenging piece of music in time for your next piano lesson. The notation may look complex, but once you take a deep breath and actually try the opening bars, you may discover that it isn't quite so hard after all, and that all you need to do is put in a few hours of practice.

If your worse fears are confirmed, and you really can't see a way of getting your work done, you are at least in a position to do something about it. For example, suppose you have to memorize approximately 100 pieces of specialist terminology in advance of an exam. You feel as though this task is overwhelming, so you keep on procrastinating. If the situation was worse than you imagined – for example, you were totally dumbfounded by the material and only had a few days in which to learn it – you could devote your time and energy to devising a strategy to help you absorb as much information as possible, or expand your study hours by canceling other engagements. If absolutely necessary, you could also contact your professor, TA, or student support service and ask for their help. Taking a proactive approach not only improves the odds that you will succeed, but it also boosts your self-image as a confident learner who is willing to take responsibility for their own success.

Assuming you know what you have to do, the next strategy to try is the five-minute rule. This is based on the principle that however boring or difficult the task, you will probably be able to tolerate it for five minutes. Tell yourself that if you feel the same way after a five-minute trial, you can stop. **Most of the time, you will find that within five minutes you will have either engaged with the task, or else you will have identified an insurmountable barrier that you will not be able to overcome in the absence of help from someone else.** Either way, you will have taken a step forward.

If the five-minute rule helps you, try variations on this technique that encourage you to work for longer periods of time. Start with ten minutes, then fifteen, and so on. The Pomodoro Technique is a great method to use when you have a daunting task ahead and need to make progress fast. It is popular in self-help circles for a good reason – it works! All you need is a timer, a piece of paper, and a pen. Set the timer for 25 minutes and start working. At the end of this period take a five-minute break. Continue working in this way until you have completed four Pomodoro periods, then rest for 20-30 minutes. The founder of this technique, Francesco

Cirillo, recommends that you make a mark on a piece of paper for each Pomodoro.[44] I can testify that it's very satisfying to see the marks build up. They serve as proof that you are making progress, and this is very encouraging.

The beauty of recording your Pomodoros is that you build up a database of how long particular tasks take. You also gain valuable insight into your overall efficiency. This helps you plan your time better in the future. For example, you may find that it takes you two Pomodoro periods to read a chapter of a textbook. Knowing that it takes you 50 minutes to read one chapter, you are in a better position to schedule your study time and organize your learning.

The Pomodoro Technique is also useful if you are studying with someone else, because it encourages both of you to keep on track. When working alongside a fellow student or colleague, it can be tempting to stop and talk rather than work. An innocent, on-topic question about the task in hand can soon develop into an irrelevant conversation. **If you agree to remain silent during each Pomodoro period and save any questions or comments for a planned break, you will both stay productive.**

Along with poor time management and a refusal to face up to a difficult task, another common cause of procrastination is resentment. Even when you know that learning is essential for your academic advancement, or even in securing a promotion, you might find yourself feeling irritable. You know that just outside your window – or just a few clicks away on your computer – there is a whole world full of more interesting things to see and do. As human beings, we want to do more of what we enjoy, and less of the things that make us frustrated and bored. That's entirely natural. In addition, we tend to find it easier to focus on what we want in the here and now, as opposed to looking into the future and predicting the consequences of our actions. There's nothing you can do to change the basic laws of human psychology, but you can make them work to your advantage.

The fact that you want to enjoy yourself isn't a problem. You shouldn't try to convince yourself that you would rather study than play a video game or hang out with your friends. In fact, you should make the most of it! Douglas Barton's research shows that the best students always make

---

[44] Cirillo Company. (2017). *Do More and Have Fun With Time Management*. Cirillocompany.de

time for fun when drawing up a study timetable. These students don't tell themselves that they are going to study 24/7, with no room for breaks. **Contrary to popular belief, the people who get the highest grades aren't actually living in their rooms or spending night after night alone in the library. The same principle holds true when it comes to the most successful entrepreneurs and their work schedules.** They know that even the most motivated, highly-focused people in the world need balanced lives if they are to enjoy peak performance.

If you don't mix some pleasure into your day, your life will shrink so that there's nothing left but work. You'll come to hate your studies, which is counterproductive. **Schedule in some enjoyable activities every day.** Each time you sit down to learn, you should know exactly when your next fun activity will be. For example, if you want to see a movie at 9 pm, write it down as part of your study schedule. It gives you a definite end point for the day, and something to look forward to. When you are in a positive frame of mind, your learning is likely to improve anyway, so it's a win-win.

Moreover, scheduling fun into your day will help you avoid falling victim to short-term distractions such as browsing social media channels, messaging your friends, and checking your email over and over again. When you know that you have something significant to look forward to later on, you'll feel more inclined to devote all your attention to your current task.

Other people like to gamify their learning. Just because a topic is serious doesn't mean you can't have some fun with it. Set yourself challenges, and have rewards on hand when you meet them. For example, if you have to make notes on three chapters from a textbook, give yourself a reward every time you complete one chapter. Be sure to follow through on the promises you make to yourself. If you cheat yourself out of the rewards you promised yourself, you won't feel so inclined to try to earn them in the future.

Remember too that procrastination, like any other destructive behavior, can be thought of as a bad habit. You might delay a task because you don't like it or believe it to be futile, but you may have procrastinated so often that it becomes your default setting. Crazy as it sounds, it's possible to get to a point at which the thought of sitting down to tackle a task well in advance of a deadline makes you feel uncomfortable! Worse, you may even have adopted the identity of "procrastinator" into your social persona. We all know someone who almost seems to brag about how late they leave their work. Procrastination is a behavioral pattern that becomes harder and harder to escape the more often you repeat it. One of the key rules of human psychology is that we train ourselves to enact the same behaviors time and time again. The more you procrastinate, the more likely you are to do so in the future.

If this sounds familiar, you need to break the habit as you would any other – by training yourself to act differently, and tolerating the discomfort that will inevitably arise as a result. The techniques in this chapter are a good start, but if procrastination has become an entrenched pattern for you, they may prove to be difficult. Break any associations you have built between your usual study space and procrastination by moving elsewhere to work. This will prevent you slipping into procrastination mode every time you take your seat.

If you can't concentrate at all, even after trying the strategies above, take a close look at your lifestyle and daily routine. Have you been getting enough sleep, limiting caffeine, and eating wholesome foods? Fatigue will drain you of concentration, so try getting a couple more hours of sleep per night if your brain has turned to mush. Eating unhealthy, sugary foods or skipping meals can result in blood sugar peaks and troughs, which can affect your cognitive abilities.

Some people find that sitting down for more than half an hour at a time makes them too restless to concentrate. There are three solutions to this problem. First, take plenty of exercise outside of study sessions, so that your body feels calm and relaxed. Second, make a point of getting up for a few minutes every hour to do a few stretches and jumping jacks. This releases pent-up energy and encourages blood flow to the brain. Third, consider investing in a standing desk. Research has shown that working in a standing position not only burns more calories than sitting, but it also boosts general productivity.[45] We all have our individual preferences when it comes to learning, and when it comes to anti-procrastination techniques, what works for someone else may do nothing for you. What might explain these differences? Psychologists aren't sure, but numerous theories have been put forward in an attempt to explain this variation. In the next chapter, we'll take a critical look at one of the most influential theories out there.

---

[45] McDonough, M. (2016). *Standing desks boost productivity, not just health, study finds.*
https://www.washingtonpost.com/lifestyle/wellness/standing-desks-boost-productivity-not-just-health-study-finds/2016/05/31/b7948390-2358-11e6-8690-f14ca9de2972_story.html?utm_term=.c537a0781844

Chapter 13: The Truth About Learning Styles

In this chapter, I'm going to talk about one of the most beloved theories of educators everywhere – the theory of learning styles. Although the concept that everyone learns in a different way makes intuitive sense, this theory is often applied in such a fashion that people become confused as to how learning really works. After outlining the key assumptions of this theory, I'm going to show you why you can safely ignore it.

Yes, that's right – despite what you may have heard, there's actually very little evidence that the concept of learning styles has any merit whatsoever. This chapter is more theoretical than others in this book, but given the popularity of learning styles theory, I knew it deserved its own section. If you've ever been tempted to go on a course based on this kind of theory, save your time and money! You are about to discover why the whole paradigm is a myth.

There are a number of variations on learning styles theory, but they tend to share one underlying premise: we all have our own distinct learning styles, which just so happen to fall into one of several categories. Most of these theories state that there are three types of learning style: visual, auditory, and kinesthetic. Some theories postulate that there may be over a dozen learning styles, but I'm going to keep things simple and focus on the most popular model.

Visual learners are said to absorb information best when it is depicted as words or pictures. Auditory learners supposedly learn best when they encounter and process information via their sense of hearing, whereas kinesthetic learners are believed to learn knowledge and skills more rapidly when they can physically move around, or link the material to their personal experiences or emotions. According to its supporters, the theory explains why some people just don't seem to grasp certain subjects or ideas. For instance, if someone claims to find reading "too hard," learning style proponents would say that they have an underdeveloped visual learning system, and that they must have an auditory or kinesthetic style instead. It's hard to teach someone how to read without relying primarily on visual aids, so according to this theory, such a person will never be a strong reader.

Learning styles theory is popular among students and workers of all ages. Aside from the fact that it jibes with our personal experience – for example, we all know some people who seem bored by visual stimuli such as movies, but love listening to music - it also validates those who find some subject areas particularly difficult. If you really suck at math, it can be comforting to have a so-called "scientific theory" to back you up. You can tell yourself and other people that you just aren't good at math because it isn't "auditory enough," so how could anyone teach it to you?

If you are struggling to get to grips with a practical task at work, telling yourself that it's "too kinesthetic" feels better than admitting that you need more practice, or that you couldn't be bothered to ask your boss for clearer instructions. **Everyone has an ego, and some of us will go to great lengths to deny that we suffer from a lack of ability, motivation, or both.** These theories are popular with teachers and parents because it seems kinder to talk about a child's ability profile in terms of learning styles, rather than with reference to their strengths and weaknesses.

The problem for those who support this theory is that, upon closer examination, it doesn't stand up to scrutiny. We'll start by thinking about learning styles in relation to certain types of skills. As education expert Ransom Patterson notes, it would be a very silly idea to try and learn to cook (a physical, kinesthetic skill) by watching cookery videos (which make use of the visual and auditory systems). If you truly want to improve your culinary expertise, you need to practice cooking. In other words, you need to make the right match between the type of material or skill you are looking to learn, and the learning style you are using in order to meet your objective.

However, you might not care much for cooking, and prefer watching videos about people preparing food. In this case, you might wish that you could learn how to make the perfect soup or roast chicken by watching video footage, but such a wish would be futile. Just because you have a particular learning preference, this doesn't mean that such a preference actually equates to better performance. There is no consistent relationship between how much a person enjoys a learning technique, and the efficacy of the approach in question.[46]

There is practically no evidence that people who exhibit certain learning styles are more likely

---

[46] Patterson, R. (2016). *Why the "Learning Styles" Concept is Wrong (And What to Use Instead)*. https://collegeinfogeek.com/learning-styles-vs-techniques/

to learn material when it is presented in a format that supposedly suits them best. **In fact, most of the research conducted on this topic shows that it's the match between the format and the material being taught that is more important in determining learning outcomes.** An individual's "learning style" has little effect on the final outcome. For example, students who practice speaking another language will make faster progress than those trying to learn it by reading notes or textbooks. In another blow to the learning styles theory, psychologists have also found that an individual's past performance in tests is much more useful in predicting their future scores than the style of teaching used by their teachers or professors.[47]

Finally, it's also worth noting that all learning styles research suffers from a basic limitation – there is no definitive test or assessment that provides a reliable indication of someone's learning style, and self-report tests are often inaccurate.[48] This isn't to say that there aren't enough learning styles tests out there. On the contrary, there are dozens. Most are sold by companies who make money from the concept by offering testing, training, and consultancy services, all of which they claim are backed up by psychological theories.

There are two further problems with learning styles theory. The first is that it cannot be used in the same way with all subjects and skills. If learning styles theory were true, there would be a lot of people out there who wouldn't stand a chance of picking up particular skills. For example, let's say a group of people were learning how to play the violin. This skill requires an individual to learn how to manipulate the violin and bow, whilst producing notes indicated on a sheet of music. Most people would agree playing the violin is primarily a kinesthetic skill, as it entails learning how to make certain movements at a particular time. There is also a strong auditory component too, because you have to listen to the feedback coming from the violin and adjust your behavior accordingly.

To a lesser extent, violinists also need to draw on their visual learning skills, because visual memory is necessary when it comes to reading music. In summary, playing the violin is a skill that must be taught using kinesthetic approaches – a student will not learn just by watching their teacher play. Is it true that the best violinists are kinesthetic learners, followed by those

---

[47] Jarrett, C. (2015). *All You Need To Know About The "Learning Styles" Myth, In Two Minutes.* https://www.wired.com/2015/01/need-know-learning-styles-myth-two-minutes/
[48] Ibid.

with strong auditory learning abilities, with primarily visual learners much worse off? There is no evidence that this is the case.

The second major point of criticism is based on the fact that research has uncovered near-universal truths about learning and memory. For example, think back to the mass and spaced repetition research in chapter 10. In one study, a group of students had to listen to a speech as it was read, and then recall it to the best of their ability at a later date. Spaced repetition was more effective than massed repetition.

The participants were not assessed for learning style, but their results all followed the same pattern. If some were auditory learners, some were visual learners, and some were kinesthetic learners – which is what you would expect if the learning styles theory were true – we wouldn't see such a uniform pattern across the whole sample. Because the information was given in spoken form, learning style theory would predict that so-called auditory learners would outperform others. Yet there was no reason to believe that the sample contained a group of auditory learners who outshone everyone else.

OK, you may be thinking, *perhaps it isn't backed up by research. But what harm can it do? If people want to think of themselves as a particular kind of learner, might this help them take a proactive approach to their studies?* **Unfortunately, these theories can promote a negative approach to learning, and can even damage self-confidence.** If you have ever taken a test designed to ascertain your personal learning style, the results may have made a lasting impression on you. If your teachers or parents were particularly enamored of such theories, you may have grown up thinking that you could only learn in one particular way.

I believe this is what makes learning style theories unhelpful. They reinforce the notion that some people are doomed to struggle in certain areas. Back in the 1960s, two psychologists conducted a study showing that when teachers expect their students to do well in school, their marks improve.[49] This study inspired other researchers to look into the mechanics of self-fulfilling prophecies.

---

[49] Rosenthal, R., & Jacobson, L. (1968). Pygmalion in the classroom. *The Urban Review, 3, 1,* 16-20.

Essentially, your personal expectations have a direct impact on your achievements. It's not unreasonable to conclude that if a teacher or professor told you that you have a particular learning style, you may internalize this information as gospel truth and adjust your expectations accordingly.

These theories do get one thing right – people certainly differ to some extent when it comes to successful learning and retention. I can't argue with that. In fact, it's one of the reasons I've included so many tips and techniques in this book. However, when it comes to the specific learning styles, there is little evidence that they actually have any real-world application. Don't waste time taking quizzes that purport to identify your learning style – they are useless.

Instead, experiment with established learning methods that have been proven to work. Learning styles theories maintain that everyone has their own preferred way of assimilating new information. Yet, somewhat ironically, they overlook the fact that everyone has their own unique genetic profile, educational background, interests, and attitudes that will combine to shape the ways in which they learn.[50]

This chapter may be a lot to take in if you have long believed yourself to show a particular learning style. However, the fact that it's a load of nonsense is actually great news! **You don't need to condemn yourself to any particular label or category. You are capable of learning in any number of ways.** Some learning techniques will work well for you, others won't. This is completely normal, and doesn't mean that you have any particular kind of "learning style." In the next chapter, we'll look at one of the most popular techniques that is primarily visual in nature, but can be used by almost anyone to great effect.

---

[50] Riener, C., & Willingham, D. (2010). The myth of learning styles. *The Magazine Of Higher Learning, 42, 5,* 32-35.

Chapter 14: How To Master Mind Mapping

When you summarize a set of ideas on a piece of paper, how do you tend to present them? Most people write notes in a linear format, in much the same style you'd expect to see in a textbook. We are taught to read words left to right, line by line, moving down a page, so it's not surprising that we replicate this layout when making notes of our own. However, this isn't always the most effective way of summarizing and learning paper-based information. **In this chapter, I'm going to tell you how to use mind maps to establish what you already know about a subject, and consolidate your knowledge.** The basic concept is pretty well-known, but many learners don't know how to construct helpful mind maps.

Let's review what mind maps are. In 1970, Tony Buzan popularized the notion that vast amounts of information can be condensed in an easily-accessible format that makes it easier for learners to review the material. A standard mind map resembles a diagram with branchlike structures radiating from a central title or keyword. Since then, this simple idea has expanded to form the basis of Buzan's company, which offers training, resources, and online software that allows students all over the world to create their own learning aids. Tony Buzan is still regarded as the leading expert on the topic. According to him, there are five basic steps you need to follow in order to create an effective mind map.[51]

First, you need to decide on your keyword, or a brief title that encapsulates the subject at hand. Don't overthink this step – your first idea will probably be good enough. For example, if you need to learn all the stages in the Krebs Cycle, simply write "Krebs Cycle" in the center of the page. Draw or paste in a small image that reminds you of the central topic. This will act as a visual trigger when you later recall the information in the rest of the map. Choose your paper size based on the complexity of the topic. The more complex the topic, the more points you will need to note down, and the more space you will require.

Next, add four or five branches. Each branch should be of a different color, and radiate from the center by at least several inches. Make sure that you leave enough room between each branch to avoid crowding the page. You can always add more branches later, but four or five is

---

[51] iMindMap. (2017). *How to Mind Map.* https://imindmap.com/how-to-mind-map/

a good number with which to start. Once you have your branches in place, add a few sub-branches. As you draw them, think about the key topics and subtopics represented by each. **Stick to the rule of one word for one branch.** The keys to a good mind map are simplicity and clear associations between concepts. Using only one word at a time keeps your map simple, and it also gives you more flexibility when forming sub-branches. Avoid using sentences or more than one word per branch, because this restricts your options as your map expands.

For example, suppose you were learning basic facts about the history of communication. If you were to write "Cellular telephone" on a branch, this would narrow subsequent sub-branches to areas related only to cell phones. However, if you wrote "Telephone" instead, you could then create branches about various types of phones, which then provides you with more scope to map out facts and figures pertaining to other major inventions that have shaped human communication.

The third step is to embrace color. Make your mind map visually engaging by coloring each main branch and its sub-branches. This encourages your brain to link particular colors with chunks of information. To continue with the example above, you might choose to color the "Telephone" branch blue, along with all its sub-branches. If you were also using the mind map to learn important facts about "Radio," this would be another main branch. You could color this branch red, thus creating a clear distinction between the two topics. As you added further sub-branches to both, you would make sure that they were appropriately colored in the same fashion.

Lastly, make small sketches or draw symbols that you associate with each topic. If you feel self-conscious about your drawing skills, feel free to print out some images and paste them onto the paper instead. You don't have to include images for every single branch, but adding a few pictures here and there will make the exercise more enjoyable, and it will encourage your brain to further process the information within the map.

So why is mind mapping effective? The first reason is that it forces you to engage with material in a proactive manner. You know that you only have a limited space in which to condense a vast amount of material. This means that you have to evaluate each piece of information in order to determine whether it warrants a place on the map. This process encourages deep learning, which aids later recall.

The second reason is that it provides you with a revision aid. A good mind map is basically a brief set of notes. **The end result is a highly portable, well-organized summary of everything you need to know.** You can then use it as the foundation of other study techniques. For example, if you want to create a set of flashcards, you could base them on the major branches of the map, ensuring that you write at least five questions that test your knowledge of each. When using the Feynman technique, you can use your mind map to quickly ascertain whether you have successfully explained the key points behind a concept, and the relationship between them.

You can even use a mind map as an especially large, detailed flashcard in its own right. Give yourself several minutes to study the mind map, then flip it over. On another piece of paper, try and recreate it in as much detail as possible. **Start by recalling the title in the center of the page, and then take yourself on a mental journey around the key branches.** At this point, you will understand why color is an important element to a successful mind map. When you form associations between colors and particular branches, you gain access to a set of powerful triggers that help you bring to mind vital facts and figures. If you get completely stuck, try to picture the sub-branches, asking yourself how many there are on your map. Push yourself further, and try to remember how each is labeled.

Once you have recalled the map to the best of your ability, compare your new version to the original. You will probably be stronger in some areas than others, and this assessment can guide you in your future study sessions. If you can't seem to get a grip on one or two areas in particular, you may need to rewrite your mind map in such a way that the links between them and the core topic are made clear.

Finally, the process of mind mapping gives you a sense of control and direction. When you create a mind map, you are setting yourself a tangible outcome – to summarize a collection of material in a clear, easy-to-read format. If you are feeling overwhelmed by the sheer amount of information you need to learn, the clarity of a mind map can be a godsend. From personal experience, I can tell you that writing a mind map is an effective way to summarize the theories of leading 20th-century sociologists, the principles of homeostasis, and probably anything else you could think of.

If you prefer to work digitally rather than with paper and pens, try a mind mapping software. iMindMap is the official software endorsed by Tony Buzan, and retails for $85. If you want to use mind mapping to plan out a large project and summarize research from many different sources, this may be an option for you. However, most of us just need to create straightforward maps that lay out the crucial points we really need to know. There are several free apps out there that allow you to do just that. They include MindMup2 (mindmup.com) and XMind (www.xmind.net). Both services offer free and paid options.

Creating an online mind map allows you to create multiple copies within seconds, which is a good insurance policy. It's reassuring to know that you have a backup if you are the kind of person who tends to spill coffee all over their notes, or lose them in the library. It also gives you the opportunity to make notes on your map. You can try new images and additional branches without having to consider the overall impact on your original diagram.

Another advantage of digital mind mapping over the traditional pen and paper method is that size isn't an issue. When you use software, you'll never run out of space. However, I'd argue that this can actually be detrimental. **For me, mind mapping is valuable because it forces me to decide which areas within a topic are really crucial to my overall understanding.**

If I have a very large piece of paper, or give myself permission to stick as many pieces together as I like, it's easy for me to use hundreds of small branches in an attempt at recording every conceivable thought I may have about a subject. I realized long ago that if I don't know how to condense information down onto a side of A2, it's either because I don't yet understand it well enough, or I'm actually trying to combine two or more topics together. Should your mind maps become unwieldy, take the biggest branch and use it as the basis for a separate mind map. Experiment to find the right number of mind maps for your specific situation. It's all part of the learning process!

At this point, you may be wondering whether there is any convincing evidence that mind maps work in accelerating learning and improving recall. **The good news is that there is evidence in support of this technique.** For example, a study focusing on recollection of factual information in a sample of medical students found that mind mapping boosted their long-term retention by ten per cent.[52] More encouraging evidence comes from work with young children, which has shown that they are more likely to remember words when they are revised using mind maps rather than conventional lists.[53]

I'd like to offer a bonus tip for those of you studying for exams. If you reread, recreate, and generally become very familiar with the contents of a mind map, you should be able to note down its key points within a couple of minutes. When you get into the exam hall, outline the main points on a blank piece of paper or in the back of your answer booklet. You can then proceed with the test, safe in the knowledge that you have already written down the key facts you are likely to need. Mind maps are also useful when planning essay answers in exam situations. Jot down the question in the center of the page, and create a major branch for each key point you need to include. Next, use sub-branches to record other facts or points that will back up your arguments. Number the branches according to the order in which you will present them in your answer, and then start writing!

Mind maps are a great technique when you need to break a vast amount of material down into manageable chunks. In the next chapter, I'll show you how to use another famous technique that will make even the most advanced topics seem manageable.

---

[52] Toi, H. (2009). Research on how Mind Mapping improves memory. Paper presented at the International Conference on Thinking, Kuala Lumpur, June 2009.
[53] Farrand, P., Hussain, F., & Hennessy, E. (2002). The efficacy of the 'mind map' study technique. *Medical Education, 36, 5,* 426-431.

Chapter 15: Powerful Mnemonic Systems That Work

It's an inescapable fact that some pieces of information are easier to recall than others. For example, you can probably remember an insulting comment made several months ago by a colleague, but may struggle to remember a list of important technical jargon. The cruel irony is that the things we so often want to remember are usually harder to recall than those we can't seem to stop thinking about! Most of us have sat in an exam or important meeting, unable to remember key points relevant to the questions or issues under discussion, yet all too able to recall the lyrics to a popular song. **In this chapter, you will learn a set of techniques that will help you make links between information that is easy for you to remember, with complex facts that are harder to recall.**

When you make use of a word, phrase, picture, acronym, or song that helps you recall something else, you are using a mnemonic device, or a mnemonic system. One of the most famous examples is that used to help children remember the colors of the rainbow – Richard Of York Gave Battle In Vain, which denotes Red, Orange, Yellow, Green, Blue, Indigo, and Violet. This is an example of an acrostic, because each word in the mnemonic phrase stands in for the first letter of the words you want to remember. Not all mnemonics spell out information quite so literally. The "Thirty days hath September" mnemonic uses rhyme and rhythm in constructing a memorable saying that helps the speaker recall the number of days in any given month.

Acronyms are another common type of mnemonic device. For example, the acronym HOMES represents the names of the five North American Great Lakes – Huron, Ontario, Michigan, Erie, and Superior. Medical students use the acronym SPAMS to help them recall the most common causes of heart murmur – Stenosis of a valve, Partial obstruction, Aneurysms, Mitral regurgitation, and Septal defects. They are useful if you need to learn technical terms, or the names of various stages within a theory. **If you can arrange the words in such a way that the resulting acronym is in some way relevant to the topic, so much the better, as this will make it even more memorable.**

You can also remember information as a specific number of letters. For example, nursing students remember the four most common precipitating factors of an angina attack with by thinking about the "4 Es" – Exertion, Eating, Emotional stress, and Extreme Temperatures. You may have to reword a piece of information to make it fit the mnemonic, but that's OK as long as it still conveys the underlying meaning. As long as you remember that correct number of letters, your brain will be able to search its memory stores and retrieve the complete set of data you need.

If you can't think of a mnemonic device of your own, there are hundreds listed online. For example, mnemonic-device.com contains lists by subject, which are free for anyone to use. **However, you'll gain the most from mnemonics if you devise your own. Exercising a bit of creativity forces you to work with the information, thus encouraging retention and recall.**

Songs are another great mnemonic device. They've been proven to work in aiding long-term recall. Big corporations know this, and take full advantage of it when marketing their products. After all, how many times have you found yourself complaining, "I can't get that stupid jingle out of my head"? When you hear new information accompanied by an engaging tune, it's more likely to enter your long-term memory. A study carried out with children and college students tested the value of a lecture versus a song in transmitting new scientific information. Participants recalled more information in the song condition, suggesting you are likely to remember facts if you can find a way of combining them with music.[54]

You don't need to be a musician to do this. Either make up new lyrics for an existing song, or look online for songs other people have devised for study purposes. The "I'm a Virus!" rap by Glenn Wolkenfeld is a superb example of the power of music in conveying scientific information, and is freely available on YouTube.[55] If you can't find a song that fits your topic, and you really want to use music as a mnemonic device, why not commission your own piece? You can find musicians who will put together a short song or rap for you on freelancing platforms such as Fiverr (fiverr.com). If you are studying as a group, you could each throw in a few dollars. If you have the time and commitment, you could also write a rap or song during a group study session. If you prefer stories to songs, why not create a story that makes use of the terms you need to

---

[54] Chazin, S., & Neuschatz, J.S. (1990). Using a Mnemonic to Aid in the Recall of Unfamiliar Information. *Perceptual and Motor Skills, 71, 3,* 1067-1071.
[55] Science Music Videos. (2012). *I'm A Virus! (Mr. W's Virus Rap).* https://youtu.be/kYf_Sl8W3qY

learn? Create a narrative that includes every word, presented in a way that makes sense to you.

For example, let's say you needed to learn the following list of words, each relating to a form of communications technology: Writing, radio, telephone, television, and internet. You could tell yourself a story that makes use of all these technologies. For example, "I got up and wrote down everything I had to do that morning. Whilst eating breakfast, I listened to the radio. Then I returned a call to my mom, who wanted to tell me about a new TV show she had seen. I hadn't seen it before, so I looked it up online." Adding visual imagery helps consolidate mnemonics, so if you were to use this example, you should picture yourself moving through the actions described in the story.

Mnemonics don't work for everyone. I've had people tell me that they just require too much time and effort. On the other hand, they seem particularly useful for those in particular disciplines. I used to work with a guy called Will. He went to medical school and worked as a physician for almost a decade. By the time I met him, he had switched careers and was working as a management consultant and executive trainer. We were talking about learning and teaching methods one day in the coffee room, and I asked him how it was that medical students managed to commit so many anatomical terms to memory.

He laughed and said, "Mnemonics, obviously! I mean, you're sunk without them." **I realized then that the type of material you are studying will play a large part in how well mnemonics will work for you.** Philosophy students probably won't find them as useful, because their subject demands a broader appreciation of the relationships between abstract ideas, whereas medicine focuses primarily on facts and in-depth technical knowledge. Then again, a creative philosopher might enjoy the challenge of representing an advanced epistemological theory as an acrostic or acronym!

Adding a little humor – even if it is dark - to your mnemonic devices will make them more effective. For instance, in order to remember the difference between cyanide and cyanate, you could use the mnemonic rhyme, "Cyanate, I ate; Cyanide, I died." To use another example with a different type of mnemonic, the acrostic, "Richard Of York Gave Battle In Vain" may be even more memorable if combined with a mental image of an inefficient general failing to fight back against his enemies. Psychologists aren't yet sure why humor seems to help us retain information.[56] It may be that humor elicits a strong emotional and even physical response (i.e., smiles and laughter), which may make it easier to recall memories at a later date. Some people swear by the peg word method, which also makes use of light-hearted ideas as memory aids. When you come across it for the first time, it may seem a little convoluted. However, research suggests that it is an effective technique that can help you recall items in a list.[57] This technique is made up of two stages:

First, you need to commit a list of ten pairs of number-rhyme combinations. The most common is the "One is a bun" version. It goes like this - "One is a bun, two is a shoe, three is a tree, four is a door, five is a hive, six is sticks, seven is Heaven, eight is a gate, nine is wine, ten is a hen." Peg systems usually contain no more than ten pegs, for the simple reason that few words rhyme with higher numbers. Once you have mastered this basic rhyme, you have access to ten "pegs." When you think of "one," you should automatically think of a bread bun, and so forth.

The next step is to combine each peg with the item you need to learn, so that you end up with a memorable visual aid. For example, suppose you have to remember a list of elements, beginning with helium, neon, and calcium. To link your first item, helium, you would need to tie it to an image of a bun. You might imagine a bun rising up into the sky, like a helium balloon, or perhaps talking in a squeaky voice.

Next, you would create a visual link between a shoe and the second element on your list, neon. A bright, neon-colored shoe could work well here. Finally, since three is a tree, you would need to think of a means of combining an image of a tree with the idea of calcium. Perhaps you could think of a tree made of chalk, or a tree that produces bottles of milk instead of fruit.

If you prefer to think in terms of simple shapes rather than vivid images, try spatial grouping methods. The first step is to identify the terms and phrases you need to remember. The second is to write them on a piece of paper in such a way that instead of forming lines or a regular column, they create shapes. Returning to the example above, you could write the names of the three elements so that they form a triangle on a piece of paper. To recall the list at later date,

---

[56] Carlson, K.A. (2011). The impact of humor on memory: Is the humor effect about humor? *International Journal of Humor Research, 24,* 1.
[57] Carney, R.N., & Levin, J.R. (2010). Delayed mnemonic benefits for a combined pegword-keyword strategy, time after time, rhyme after rhyme. *Applied Cognitive Psychology, 25, 2,* 204-211.

you could think of a triangle, which would then prompt you to remember each of the three elements.[58]

Although some of these methods may seem strange or unhelpful, research shows that they can definitely work for some of us. So how do mnemonic devices boost learning and recall? The main reason is that they allow you to focus on recalling a single piece of information rather than a long list of facts, which in turn can be "unpacked" to reveal more ideas. We all know that recalling a single piece of information is easier than recalling a long list of facts. A mnemonic is therefore a shortcut, a means of accessing a web of information.[59] Putting together mnemonics also encourages you to develop a deeper understanding of a topic, because you need to sift through the information in order to develop a device that works in conveying the key points. Mnemonics make studying more fun, which in turn can increase your motivation and overall enjoyment.

However, they are not a magic wand. It isn't enough to devise a mnemonic and then hope that your brain will access it during a test. **You will need to rehearse it during your practice exams, and by testing yourself to ensure that you recall both the contents of your mnemonic and what it stands for.** It's also important to note that you can become bogged down in mnemonics if you attempt to condense everything you need to learn down into memorable phrases, acronyms, or acrostics. **Save mnemonic techniques for specific pieces of information that are hard to recall on their own.** They should supplement your usual learning techniques, not serve as a replacement.

You should also bear in mind that a well-chosen mnemonic will stick with you for years to come, so make sure that it's an image you want to live with! Basing a mnemonic on something negative or gruesome might well make it more memorable, but there's a high probability that whenever someone makes reference to the topic in the future, your brain will dredge up that memory. Aim to make your mnemonics as fun as possible.

The mnemonics described in this chapter are useful if you need to learn short or medium-length

---

[58] Mohammad, A., & Ketabi, S. (2015). Mnemonic Instruction: A Way to Boost Vocabulary Learning and Recall. *Journal of Language Teaching and Research, 2, 1,* 178-182.
[59] Ibid.

lists of information. However, they are less helpful if you need to remember the relationships between various concepts, or if you need to memorize a long list of words and phrases. In the next chapter, we'll look at a technique that allows you to learn a vast amount of information - the method of loci.

Chapter 16: The Method Of Loci

In the previous chapter, you learned several techniques that can help you commit information to memory via mnemonics. However, I've dedicated a separate chapter to the oldest, perhaps most famous mnemonic approach of them all – the method of loci. You'll discover the history behind the technique, the situations in which it is most effective, and how to make it work for you.

Historians and psychologists alike believe that people have been using the method of loci for thousands of years. The word "loci" means "locations" in Latin, a reference to the role played by actual or imaginary locations in helping those using this technique to recall pieces of information. It is sometimes known as the "journey method," or the "mind palace method."

Ancient Greek and Roman orators would often give lengthy speeches, which could last for many hours, without the use of notes. They knew that they wouldn't possibly be able to remember a speech word for word, but they wanted to ensure that they didn't omit any crucial details. Paper was not widely available, and it was unacceptable to merely read a speech. These societies judged someone on the basis of their oratory abilities, as well as the quality of their arguments. Therefore, an unobtrusive, reliable memory technique was required.

No one knows who first wrote about the method of loci. The earliest recorded instance is found in a text entitled "Rhetorica ad Herennium," produced around 80 B.C by an anonymous writer. However, we do know that other individuals adopted it. The Roman politician Cicero used the method of loci, and recommended it to those looking to become powerful speakers.

It has several applications. You can use the method of loci to commit facts to memory. However, you can also use it for its original purpose – structuring a speech and then delivering it without the aid of notes or slides. This will always impress an audience, as it implies that you are so familiar with the material that you need no external prompting. You can even make use of it in your personal life. Have you ever had to prepare for a difficult discussion with a family member or friend, in which you knew you would have to make several important points whilst keeping a cool head? The method of loci can help you make a coherent argument under pressure.

The method of loci depends on making associations between places (loci) and ideas. **You first need to decide on an imaginary route.** Roman speakers would prepare for their speeches by mentally rehearsing the act of walking through their town or city. Once they had chosen their route, they would go over it several times, establishing the locations they would pass and the order in which they would pass them.

An orator would then conjure up images that represented the points they wanted to make in their speech, ensuring that each location was represented by a single image. For example, if they decided to begin their speech by talking about the state of the local economy, they may have imagined a bag of coins on the front steps leading up to their house. When standing up to begin their speech, they would begin their mental walk at home, where the sight of the coins would serve as an effective prompt to start talking about local trade.[60]

Take a moment now to choose the route you will use. Close your eyes and imagine that you are making the journey right now, in real time. What landmarks do you see along the way? The word "landmark" is often used to denote a special point of interest, but it can include mundane places, such as a grocery store or set of traffic lights. Make a list of these landmarks. It doesn't matter how far apart they are. As long as they are distinct from one another, and you know in which order they occur as you continue on your journey, you should include them in your route.

If you find it hard to visualize your path, pay special attention the next time you take it. Sometimes, we go on autopilot mode and ignore our surroundings. Make a resolution to start paying close attention in the future. Within a few days, you should be able to access the memory of how it feels to move along the route.

Alternatively, you could use your home as your "route." The main advantage here is that you are likely to be more familiar with your home than any other place, so you won't have to think too hard when recalling it. However, unless you live in an enormous house, there are likely to be only a few rooms you can use as landmarks along your mental pathway. This means that a home-based route is unlikely to be useful for anything other than relatively short lists. It's best to memorize two routes you can use – one within your home, and one outside it. Both should

---

[60] Frakt, A. (2016). *An Ancient and Proven Way to Improve Memorization; Go Ahead and Try it.*
https://www.nytimes.com/2016/03/24/upshot/an-ancient-and-proven-way-to-improve-memory-go-ahead-and-try-it.html

offer you the maximum possible number of landmarks. It is important that you "visit" the landmarks in the same order every time you rehearse the route in your head.

The next step is to tie each piece of information you need to recall to a landmark along your mental route, taking into account the order in which you need or want to retrieve it. Sometimes, the order will not matter – for instance, if you are learning a list of endangered species, order is probably irrelevant – but if you are committing to memory a model or sequence of events, make sure that you factor this in when setting out your landmarks.

For example, if you are learning the order of the elements in the periodic table, you would first need to recall hydrogen, then helium, then lithium. If you are using a home-based route, your first three landmarks might be your front door, your hallway, and your utility room. You could imagine hydrogen as water, cascading down your front door like a waterfall. As you enter the hallway, you may find that you start talking in a squeaky voice, due to the presence of helium.

You may then envisage yourself entering the utility room, where you see a huge bottle of pills – lithium tablets. Obviously, these are just examples I have come up with whilst writing this chapter. The beauty of this method is that you can customize it to suit your needs and imagination. **Finally, you need to practice moving through your house or along your route until you can instantly "see" the images that trigger relevant pieces of information.**

Unlike many other mnemonic devices, the method of loci has no limits regarding the amount of information you can commit to memory. Acronyms can only be so long before they become too hard to remember, and peg systems typically accommodate only ten words at a time. However, the number of items you can recall using the method of loci is constrained only by the number of locations you can recall at once. If you base your imaginary walk on a route you take on a regular basis, you will have potentially dozens of landmarks at your disposal. **Bear in mind too that you don't have to envisage walking the entirety of a route – if you normally use a train, bus, or car, you can incorporate those too.**

There is plenty of scientific evidence to support the basic principles behind this method. Psychologists have long emphasized the power of imagery. When you enter a new place, especially if you are there for a significant event such as a job interview or large party, you leave with a huge number of new memories. For example, even a few days, weeks, or months after an event, you will be able to recall the overall structure and atmosphere of someone's home.

Researchers have demonstrated that our ability to differentiate between pictures of previously presented and novel objects far exceeds what most of us imagine to be possible. Amazingly, the average person can be exposed to several thousand pictures within a relatively short space of time, yet still be able to discern between those they have and have not seen when given a memory test. In another study, researchers presented participants with images of ten items, followed by pictures of 402 other objects. Participants were often able to describe the original ten images, despite having been distracted by a copious amount of unrelated information.[61]

There is also a sound piece of evolutionary theory that may go some way in explaining why visual methods work so well. As we evolved, we would have needed to know which plants and flowers were good to eat, and which would kill us. If our ancestors got it wrong, they would get sick or die. Therefore, we needed to develop an ability to recognize objects and commit images to memory so that we could call on them in the future. It also makes sense that we would develop the ability to commit routes across a variety of terrains to memory.

As hunter-gatherers, we would have needed to learn where the best hunting grounds were so that we could use our hunting time more efficiently on future trips. In light of this theory, it should come as no surprise that there are no physical differences between the brains of "normal" people and those of world-class memory champions.[62] We are all born with the same basic brain structure.

You can make the method of loci even more effective by incorporating humor and bizarre imagery. However, there is a fine line between using strange imagery to make an idea more memorable, and overloading your memory with odd images which make no sense. **Images that are too contrived and surreal actually become harder to remember.** You need to use what psychologists refer to as "minimally counterintuitive concepts," or MCCs, when

---

[61] Ibid.
[62] Ibid.

putting together your route.

In brief, MCC theory states that when an object or idea violates only one or two of our everyday expectations, it becomes pretty hard to forget.[63] On the other hand, when it becomes just too weird, it will fade quite quickly. This theory has been used to explain why talking animals are so appealing and memorable as characters – animals are "normal," but when they violate a single expectation (i.e. "animals can't talk"), they become appealing. However, a robotic, talking, ghostlike, depressed dog is a less memorable concept – it is just too weird.

So what does this mean for you? **Keep your imagery striking but simple.** To return to the example above, water cascading over a door is a surreal image that hits just the right level of weirdness. The idea of walking through your hallway, only to start talking in a squeaky voice, is also appropriate – we can all imagine speaking, but suddenly talking in a strangely high-pitched voice slightly violates our expectations.

Setting up a mental route and thinking up various images can be time-consuming, but there are published scientific reports out there attesting to the remarkable power of this technique. For example, it has been used in research settings as a means of training those of average memory capacity to recall strings of digits up to 90 numbers in length.[64]

However, there are relatively few peer-reviewed papers available on this topic. This is because the method requires time and practice to get right – often a couple of hours – so undertaking trials with groups of participants is often impractical. Another problem is that everyone will use a different route, and so it is impossible to directly compare outcomes across individuals.

A group of Canadian researchers have found that presenting participants with virtual environments might be a good solution, because everyone in a study will be using exactly the same imagery. These findings may mean that we will see an increase in research examining the mechanics of the method of loci in years to come.[65] It might also mean that if you spend a lot of

---

[63] Norenzayan, A., Atran, S., Faulkner, J., & Schaller, M. (2006). Memory and Mystery: The Cultural Selection of Minimally Counterintuitive Narratives. *Cognitive Science, 30,* 531-553.
[64] Kliegl, R., Smith, J., Heckhausen, J., & Baltes, P.B. (1987). *Cognition and Instruction, 4, 4.*
[65] Legge, E.L.G., Madan, C.R., Ng, E.T., & Caplan, J.B. (2012). Building a memory palace in minutes: Equivalent memory performance using virtual versus conventional environments with the Method of Loci. *Acta Psychologica, 141,* 380-390.

time in a virtual environment, such as an open-world game or Second Life, picturing yourself taking a path through that world might be just as effective as using a route you use in reality!

The method of loci uses the principle of location-based triggers to boost recall – you come across a mental landmark and the extra image you have added, and your brain retrieves the relevant information. In the next chapter, I'll talk about the role of context and cues in a more general sense.

Chapter 17: Environmental Context & Cues – Are They Important Factors In Your Learning?

When you learn a piece of information, you don't learn it in isolation. This observation has lead students and psychologists alike to speculate on the role played by environmental cues in memory and recall. Unfortunately, the overall picture is a little confusing, and most people aren't sure how and why it all works. In this chapter, I'm going to provide you with an overview of what we know about the effect of environment and context on the recollection and recognition of information.

If you have ever returned to a place from your childhood and been surprised to discover that you can recall more memories than you expected, you have experienced environmental context-dependent (EC) memory for yourself. Many of our memories are bound by surrounding contextual cues – we struggled to recall them if they are not present. Have you ever bumped into one of your professors or coworkers at the grocery store or gym, but failed to recognize them for a few seconds? This isn't a sign of a failing memory.

Rather, it's a sign that you have learned about their appearance in one context (college or the workplace), and your brain has difficulty in locating this same information when the cue (the person's face) is presented in a new environment.[66] A key feature of EC memory is that it occurs unconsciously. For example, no one sits in a lecture theater and decides that they will remember their professor's face in class, but be unable to recognize them in other contexts.

We have evolved to pick up on subtle environmental cues, and encode them for use at a later date. Spending a prolonged time in a particular environment allows you to build up a number of cues, which trigger one another when you experience the environment again in the future. This is why returning to your hometown will serve as a trigger for a significant number of childhood memories.

A famous study applied this principle to intentional learning. University of Stirling

---

[66] Smith, S.M. (1988). Environmental Context-Dependent Memory. In G.M. Davies & D.M. Thomson (Eds.)., *Memory in Context,* pp.13-33. Chichester: John Wiley & Sons.

psychologists David Godden and Alan Baddeley recruited a group of divers, and asked them to learn word lists in two environments: under the water, and on dry land. The divers were later asked to recall the lists in either the same environment in which they learned the material, or in the alternative setting. The results were clear – the divers performed better when they were asked to recall word lists in the same setting in which they had originally learned them.[67]

These results lead educational psychologists to wonder whether students should make a special effort to study in conditions similar to those they expect to experience in an exam. Iowa State University researchers asked 40 students to read an article in either silent or noisy conditions. They then sat two types of test – a short-answer exam (which tested their ability to recall material), and a multiple-choice test (which assessed their ability to distinguish between, and recognize, information). Students in the matching conditions – those who were tested in a similar environment to that in which they had read the article – performed significantly better on both tests. **The authors of the study concluded that if a student wants to perform well in an exam, they should study in silence.**

By extension, since you are not usually allowed to eat or drink anything other than water in an examination hall, it's probably a good idea to avoid eating or drinking whilst studying. You should also consider studying in the presence of other people, because you will be surrounded by students when you come to sit the exam. According to the results of the study, you should aim to replicate exam conditions as closely as possible.[68]

However, some people cannot bear to study in silence, and find the process easier if they play music or binaural beats. **I'm a firm believer that if there's a choice to be made between studying with music playing in the background or not studying at all, you should pick the former.** You can always make the transition to silence if you want to see how well the principles of EC learning work for you. Of course, if you are going to be assessed in a noisy environment, which may be the case if you are studying a more hands-on subject such as communication or counseling skills, learning in silence is unlikely to help you!

Unfortunately, most students cannot study for an exam in the same room in which they will

---

[67] Godden, D.R., & Baddeley, A.D. (1975). Context-dependent memory in two natural environments: on land and underwater. *British Journal of Psychology, 66, 3,* 325-331.
[68] Grant, H.M., Bredahl, L.C., Clay, J., Ferrie, J., Groves, J.E., McDorman, T.A., & Dark, V.J. (1998). Context-Dependent Memory for Meaningful Material: Information for Students. *Applied Cognitive Psychology, 12,* 617-623.

actually take the assessment. Luckily, along with external environmental cues, research shows that internally generated triggers can also serve as effective triggers that can help us recall information. **In other words, conjuring up a mental image of the place in which you learned an idea can help you remember it.** We all have the ability to visualize. If you didn't have this ability, you wouldn't be able to recognize your coat, your front door, or your best friend! Trust me when I say that you can definitely learn how to conjure up a mental image of a library, your bedroom, or wherever else you carried out the majority of your exam preparation.

If you are skeptical, consider how this principle works in everyday settings. When eyewitnesses are asked to describe what they have heard or seen, they are often encouraged to "think back" to the event in question. This acts as a memory trigger. Their internally generated cues prompt them to relive the experience all over again, and this can help them recall more information. In clinical psychology, this concept also explains why people with post-traumatic stress disorder (PTSD) suffer from flashbacks, intrusive thoughts, and panic attacks whenever they encounter a relevant trigger. For example, war veterans with PTSD are often triggered by loud noises, because they remind them of gunfire and other sounds heard in war zones. All of the above observations suggest that thinking about the place in which you studied specific material should help improve your recollection.

However, the picture becomes slightly more complicated when you review other studies published in this field, some of which have found that the EC memory effect only applies to recall-based tests, not those that depend on recognition. **In other words, EC memory is useful if you are answering short-answer or essay-type exam questions, but when it comes to multiple-choice questions, it won't help.**[69]

One of the most popular explanations for this effect is the outshining hypothesis. When we have pieces of information in front of us that we can recognize – as is the case on multiple-choice tests, whereby one of the answers is correct - we are confronted with a cue that is stronger than anything in our environment.[70] Such a cue overpowers relatively subtler environmental cues,

---

[69] Ibid.
[70] Ibid.

effectively drowning them out. At the same time, other research indicates that this effect is not consistently seen in peer-reviewed studies. It's enough to make your head hurt!

In my opinion and experience, it's worth assuming that EC memory retrieval works in both recall and recognition tests. Given that it doesn't take much effort to experiment with EC memory retrieval, why not give it a try? If you study for a multiple-choice exam in quiet exam conditions, for example, you will not have put yourself at a disadvantage, even if the outshining hypothesis means that your approach makes no difference in the end.

So far, we've looked at common environmental cues, such as physical location and background noise. However, scents are also useful when studying. Take a moment to think about the smells that have particular meaning for you. For example, the smell of freshly-baked gingerbread might take you back to the times you visited your grandmother as a young child, whilst the smell of a certain cologne may remind you of your father.

You can use the power of fragrance to trigger recall in examination settings. **A study published in the *American Journal of Psychology* demonstrated that odor cues can help students recall lists of information.**[71] This means that if you smell an odor as you learn a piece of information, smelling the odor again when you try to recall it can improve your performance. To try this for yourself, buy a new body spray or perfume. Put it on immediately prior to studying a topic that you need to recall in the future. Take a shower afterwards so that your brain learns to associate specific knowledge with the smell. When you study the same material again, or need to recall it in an exam situation, apply the scent again.

This trick is no substitute for rigorous learning techniques, but it's backed up by research and won't do you any harm. If you don't want to use a deodorant or perfume, essential oils are another option. Simply add a couple of drops to your wrist before studying a particular topic, and then apply it again just prior to your exam. Not only are these oils inexpensive, but there are also dozens of varieties available, all of which can be easily distinguished from one another. This means that you have plenty of scope for developing all the knowledge-odor associations you could reasonably need. In theory, burning candles or incense would also work, but this isn't

---

[71] Herz, R. (1997). Emotion experienced during encoding enhances odor retrieval cue effectiveness. *The American Journal of Psychology, 110, 4*, 489-505.

practical if you hope to pass a test on the subject – it's unlikely that an invigilator will allow you to bring your favorite joss sticks into an examination hall.

When I was in college, I wasn't aware that psychologists had researched the relationship between odors and learning. However, I worked out that when I wore the same shirt two days running when studying my history notes, recalling the material seemed a little easier next time around. I didn't want to keep wearing the same shirt day after day, so started to think about what else I could wear – and hit upon deodorant.

That semester, I used three different fragrances, one for each of my most difficult history topics. I was amazed to find that they really did give me an edge in tests and exams. In my working life, I like to apply my "speaking scent" whilst practicing a presentation, and then I use it again on the day of my talk. It gives my brain a little nudge, which can make all the difference in successful recall.

Interestingly, your mood also plays a role in odor-based recollection. The author of the study outlined above found that when people are anxious, they are more susceptible to the effects of odors in encoding and retrieving information.[72] This may mean that allowing yourself to remain in a state of stress whilst studying might make the odor trick more effective. However, I wouldn't recommend that you deliberately cultivate a stressed mood, if for no other reason than it isn't much fun.

There is a simple neurological explanation underlying the odor effect. The olfactory bulb, which is responsible for passing information about the odors you are smelling to the brain, is very closely connected to parts of the limbic system associated with strong emotion. This is why a mere whiff of an odor that holds special significance for us is enough to trigger powerful memories.

Odor holds a special place in the heart of memory researchers, because studies show time and time again that it is a trigger more consistently effective than color, sound, and other contextual cues. Memory is a difficult phenomenon to measure, because

---

[72] Ibid.

everyone experiences it differently. It is hard to control every possible context-based variable in laboratory conditions.

Therefore, the most sensible conclusion we can draw from the research is that although context can help you learn material in certain situations, your proficiency in various study techniques is more important. In the next chapter, we'll look at an efficient study method that doesn't enjoy the recognition it deserves, yet has the power to double your performance on tests.

Chapter 18: Interleaved Practice – How To Polish Your Skills Quickly

Accelerated learning is all about making the best use of your time. You need to hone in on the skills that will help you absorb information rapidly, and consolidate new knowledge within hours or days rather than months or years. It's important to understand not only what you need to do, but the order in which you need to get it done.

In this chapter, I'm going to teach you why most of us tend to work through our tasks in a particular order, and why this approach may not be the best use of our time. You will discover an alternative approach that will rapidly increase your knowledge acquisition. This method is particularly effective if you are studying math, science, or any other subject that requires you to make use of the same processes over and over again.

When faced with the prospect of learning several new processes, most people tackle them one after the other, as though they were a tutor guiding their students through a class syllabus. This makes sense, because it's what feels right and "normal." Most of us receive our education in blocks. For instance, let's say you are taking a class in statistics. In the first class, you might study t-tests. In the next class, you might study how to calculate a correlation coefficient, and so on.

From our earliest years in school, we are told that the best way to learn a subject is by breaking it down into small chunks and then studying them one at a time. We learn that we should make sure we have a grasp of the basic concepts, work through some easy exercises, then tackle some harder exercises, and then move onto the next "chunk." The rationale is that, over time, we will gradually expand our knowledge of the subject as a whole. This approach is termed "block practicing."

There is another way to rehearse your skills – interleaved practice. To continue with the example above, you might answer some questions on t-tests following the t-test lecture, questions on correlations following a class on the topic, and so on. This would be an example of blocked practice. However, what if you were to work through a mixture of questions on a range of statistical topics between classes? This approach is known as interleaved practice. Skills are not rehearsed in isolation. They are, quite literally, mixed in with others within the same broad subject area.

Psychologists have begun to question the wisdom of block practicing, particularly in relation to math skills. A growing body of evidence suggests that interleaved practice can be a much more effective way of testing and refining an individual's skills.

For example, a group of researchers from the University of South Florida set out to discover whether a group of 140 seventh-grade students would achieve higher scores on math tests following a period of interleaved practice. The students were split into two groups. One group received nine weeks of conventional teaching, with homework that asked them to apply the knowledge they had learned in class just prior to the assignment. The other group learned the same material, but their homework assignments featured a mix of problems. The students learned four kinds of problem in total. Prior to the experiment, none of them were familiar with the material.

Following the nine-week teaching period, the students were asked to take a surprise test. The results were astonishing. **The students who had received traditional homework assignments scored an average of 38% on the test, whereas those who had undertaken interleaved practice achieved an average of seventy-two per cent.** Although all the students had spent exactly the same amount of time learning the material, and the same amount of time practicing it, the structure of their practice made a huge difference to the final outcome.[73]

This study used a diverse range of math problems, but other experiments have demonstrated that interleaved practice also works well with tasks that are somewhat alike. This means that you can use it to good effect if you need to improve your performance on, for example, various types of algebraic equations that share some superficial similarities. However, interleaved practice would also work well if you needed to practice solving algebraic equations and quadratic equations.

So what might explain the power of interleaved practice? The authors of the study outlined

---

[73] Rohrer, D., Dedrick, R.F., & Burgess, K. (2014). The benefit of interleaved mathematics practice is not limited to superficially similar kinds of problems. *Psychonomic Bulletin & Review, 21,* 1323-1330.

above point out that when you mix problems together, you are asking your brain to switch between strategies as you move through the set. In block practice, you typically locate a single strategy, then use it to solve all the problems.

However, when you switch the material around so that no two consecutive problems can be solved using the same strategy, you are forcing your brain to do a bit more work. **Instead of applying what has worked for the previous two, three, or more problems, it has to undertake a search for the correct process each and every time. These searches essentially act as repetitions that consolidate learning.** Therefore, there are two key components in interleaved practice: problems are interleaved with others of a different kind, and problems of the same type are presented at intervals, rather than in blocks.[74]

At this point, you might be wondering whether the apparent effects of interleaving just come down to the fact that if you switch between several different topics, you are by default forcing yourself to wait before practicing each the next time around. We've already established earlier in this book that spaced practice is a great strategy for improving retention of material. However, research shows that the effects of interleaving cannot be attributed merely to spacing. Further experiments from the University of South Florida have demonstrated that interleaving offers a massive performance boost independent of the time between each practice session.[75]

What does all this research mean for you? If you are taking a math class, the implications are straightforward. When you practice solving math problems, do not work through a batch of one type of problem before moving onto the next. Write out several examples of each type on notecards, then shuffle them up. You'll find that it's harder to solve a problem when you have to consciously choose the correct strategy each and every time, but it will accelerate your learning. You may need to focus on one kind of problem at a time at first, but as soon as you have a basic grasp of what you need to do, start basing your study around interleaved practice. The fact that interleaved practice offers benefits in addition to spacing suggests that even if you are only trying to learn one skill or topic, you should add another – whether you have to or not! After all, you cannot swap between two topics or types of problem unless you are working with

---

[74] Ibid.
[75] Taylor, K., & Rohrer, D. (2010). The Effects of Interleaved Practice. *Applied Cognitive Psychology, 24,* 837-848.

diverse material. If you have sufficient time, break up your study sessions by trying to tackle problems of a very different type.

Interleaved practice also improves your ability to make distinctions between similar concepts. **You may also be interested to know that interleaved practice is also an effective strategy for those learning motor skills, such as shooting hoops or perfecting a golf swing.** For example, baseball players get better at hitting various types of pitches if their practice is interleaved in training sessions, rather than blocked.[76] If you want to improve your sporting performance, don't repeat the same focused drills over and over again for hours at a time. Complete a few repetitions, then move onto a new movement or action.

Interleaved practice can even help you understand abstract concepts and spot patterns you may fail to identify at a conscious level. In one fascinating experiment, two psychologists showed two groups of people some paintings created by a dozen artists. Both groups of participants saw the artists' names alongside their paintings. However, one group saw the paintings blocked according by artist, whereas exposure to the paintings was interleaved for the other group.

Following exposure, all participants were asked to look at another set of paintings – this time, without being able to see the names of the artists who had created them – and told to guess which of the artists had produced the pieces.

Participants in the interleaved learning group were significantly more likely to correctly match the artists with their works. This suggests that although interleaving has been primarily associated with math and physical activities, this approach can also be useful for those who want to learn how "rules" (in this case, how an artist tends to style their work) generalize across situations.[77] If you are studying art, design, or another visual subject, interspersing your exposure to the works of one individual with works of another should improve your understanding of both, even if you can't quite articulate why.

---

[76] Ibid.
[77] Ibid.

Although it enjoys plenty of empirical support, interleaving should not be used in isolation in all contexts. For example, if you are preparing for an exam, you still need to use practice papers. Although interleaved practice promotes retention, it is no substitute for solid test-taking skills. You should also use this method with care if you are easily distracted. Setting up an interleaved practice session can be a lengthy exercise if you allow yourself to get caught up in details such as the number of questions you should include on each topic, whether topics are sufficiently dissimilar, and so on. Give yourself a maximum amount of time to spend on choosing your questions and arranging your topics so that they are interleaved.

Don't worry if you feel as though you cannot recall quite as much information as usual during your study session. It's normal for students undertaking interleaved practice to remember less information than those engaged in blocked practice whilst in the midst of practicing, and immediately afterwards. **The good news is that interleaved practice usually results in better test performance a few days later!** Don't assume that the material is too difficult for you, or that you are not learning anything just because you feel challenged during a study session. In fact, if you are using the interleaved approach, you should consider it a positive sign.

Have fun mixing up questions and problems. Not only does interleaved practice help you learn faster, it also adds an element of novelty. This keeps your study sessions interesting, which will help sustain your concentration for longer periods of time. Interleaved practice is also good basis for a group learning session. For example, you could ask a study partner to combine questions for you in such a way that you end up with an especially challenging set of problems. In the next chapter, we'll take a closer look at how studying with others can work to your advantage.

Chapter 19: Accelerated Learning As Part Of A Group

If you are an extrovert, or just want to experiment with learning methods that don't entail spending a lot of time alone, you can try forming a learning group. In this chapter, we'll look at the benefits and drawbacks of learning with other people. **You'll learn how to set up a group, how to handle the problems and tensions that may arise, and how to apply some of the techniques you have learned in this guide to group sessions.** I set up a study group with three of my classmates in college, and the four of us studied for our sociology finals together. We all got great grades, and it made me wonder why I hadn't tried to work with other students on previous occasions. Unless you need absolute silence in which to concentrate, I recommend giving it a try. For reasons I will explain later in the chapter, it can help you learn a lot of material in a short space of time.

First of all, you need to think about how you will recruit group members. Your first impulse might be to ask your friends to join you. It seems logical to study with the people you like, doesn't it? Unfortunately, unless your friends are of a certain type, they might not be your best option. In their online guide to group study, Brigham Young University's Center for Teaching and Learning recommends that you select people based on their in-class behaviors.[78] This means approaching students who turn up on time, take notes, pay attention to what the professor is saying, and appear motivated to do well. It doesn't matter whether you actually like these people – they are probably perfect study buddies. Be suspicious if a lazy student seems interested in joining your group; they probably think that they can coast along on the back of other people's efforts.

Keep the group size to a maximum of six. In large groups, there is an increased risk that members will distract one another, and people are more likely to feel as though they can minimize their contributions. If other people ask to join, suggest that you divide into two distinct groups instead. Meet in a quiet location with minimal distractions, and plenty of room in which to spread out your books and notes. Avoid trying to work in someone's kitchen or bedroom. Some libraries have rooms or study pods set aside for group work. This kind of setting can be ideal, as they have a somewhat "formal" feel that encourages concentration. My college

---

[78] BYU Center for Teaching & Learning. (2017). *How to Organize and Conduct Effective Study Groups.* http://ctl.byu.edu/how-organize-and-conduct-effective-study-groups

library didn't have study pods, but we were usually able to find an empty teaching room in which to work. If you aren't sure whether there are any suitable rooms nearby, ask your professor or TA.

So what should you actually do during group sessions? **In your first session, decide on the material to be covered in the upcoming days, weeks, or even months.** If you are preparing for an assessment, the course syllabus or list of lecture topics is a good place from which to begin. Divide up the material so that everyone is responsible for leading a discussion on at least one topic. Even if someone is shy, they are not exempt from taking their turn! All group members should share the workload equally. If the math doesn't quite work out – for example, there are six topics to be covered, and four members of the group – you might have to toss a coin to decide on who takes on the extra work. Dumping too much work on one person's shoulders is a sure-fire recipe for resentment. **Make it clear from the outset that everyone will be expected to participate.**

Each session should be no longer than three hours. Most people find it hard to concentrate for a longer period of time, thus rendering the process inefficient beyond this point. Start with a 30-minute discussion on the topic, which should be lead by the appointed member of the group. They should come prepared with their own summary of the main points to be covered, along with some thought-provoking study questions.

These questions should not just be dry and factual; they should tap into the "whys" of a subject, allowing everyone in the group to get a broader perspective of the topic. For example, if the group is studying microbes as part of a biology class, the discussion leader could include questions such as, "If we didn't have antibiotics available, how would microbes affect the global population?" At the same time, it is important to keep the session on track. At the outset, nominate someone to steer the group back on course if they begin to diverge down an irrelevant path.

Note that just because a specific member of the group has been designated as discussion leader, this doesn't mean that other members can come unprepared. **If the discussion is to be of any use, everyone needs to arrive ready to share their thoughts.** Otherwise, the discussion will come to a grinding halt pretty quickly, and the discussion leader will feel as though they have wasted their time.

Writing, completing, and providing feedback on test questions is another great use of your study session. After the initial discussion period, it's time to consolidate your learning and get some test practice in at the same time. Devote the next 30 minutes to devising questions that mimic the test you will be taking. It doesn't matter whether you or other group members personally prefer one format over the other – the format will be dictated by the assessment involved! The aim is to practice responding to a particular kind of question. Set a minimum number of questions that every group member should write within the first 30 minutes.

The next 30 to 60 minutes of the session should be devoted to asking and answering the questions. The easiest way to do this is by photocopying or printing copies of the questions for everyone. Once the time period has elapsed, have everyone swap answers so that they can be marked for accuracy. Group members should then provide one another with feedback, asking any clarifying questions if necessary.

If the exam questions will be in long-answer format, staging a full-length practice test within the space of a single group session won't be practical. However, you can still challenge one another to note down the main points they would cover when writing an exam answer. You could also bring copies of extended essay exam questions you may have written in your individual study sessions, and get feedback from your fellow group members.

Finally, the original discussion leader should wrap up the session by summarizing the main points of the subject covered within the learning period. This is also an opportunity to talk about how well the group is operating as a whole, and whether members are providing one another with constructive feedback. You can also use the final few minutes to make copies of notes and practice answers for any group members who would like them.

I've just outlined a schedule that worked pretty well for me in my college days, but of course there are other formats you could try, and other group activities that may be of use. For example, you could begin the session by watching a few brief video clips on the subject, and basing your discussion around those. You could also begin with a flashcard game, whereby one person takes on the role of quizmaster, challenging everyone else to gain as many points as possible! Feel free to get creative. However, do not lose sight of your key aim – to join together in furthering your knowledge, and learning how to process information on a particular topic.

So how exactly can this approach help you? **A study group can accelerate your learning because it forces you to focus.** When you are seated around a table with several other people, you can't just slack off and play video games. The peer pressure and social norms that come with group interactions will keep you engaged with the learning process even when you would have quit were you to study alone. If you have chosen your fellow group members well, you'll be spending time with some high achievers. This can ignite your competitive spirit, which will boost your motivation. It's pretty satisfying to show off your hard-earned knowledge!

You will also benefit from picking up study tips from others, and this can save you time. All the accelerated learning techniques you will ever need are contained within this book. However, some methods will work better for some subjects than others. Your study buddies may be able to tell you what they have found to be especially useful in their exam preparation.

Now you know the benefits of learning in a group, but what about the drawbacks? You won't be surprised to learn that psychologists have undertaken plenty of research into group dynamics. Anyone who has worked as part of a group at school or within a team at work knows that sometimes, it just doesn't work out.

The first problem is slacking. It's common for one person to put in noticeably less effort than everyone else, even if they claim that they have joined the group with the intention of working hard and engaging with everyone else. In psychological jargon, this phenomenon is known as "social loafing." Social loafing is a big problem, because it doesn't just reduce the loafer's performance – it also lowers group morale.[79] It's frustrating to spend hours preparing for a discussion, or thinking of questions to ask other group members, only to realize that one or two people aren't putting in any effort.

Telling someone that they are slacking off and contributing very little of value is likely to cause

---

[79] Karau, S.J., & Williams, K.D. (1993). Social Loafing: A Meta-Analytic Review and Theoretical Integration. *Journal of Personality and Social Psychology, 65, 4,* 681-706.

arguments. **When it comes to loafing, prevention is better than cure.** Conscientious people who are motivated to work are less likely to indulge in loafing, so pick your group with care. **You could also create a set of group rules during your first session.** For example, what will happen to those who do not pull their weight? How many times can a member turn up late or ill-prepared and still be permitted to attend the next session?

Discussing group rules may feel awkward, but all sensible participants will recognize the value of laying down a set of shared expectations. In fact, holding a formal meeting to decide what members of the group can expect from one another is an effective means of weeding out those who are likely to loaf, because you are making it clear from the start that slacking will not be tolerated.

Another issue you may come up against is groupthink.[80] First observed by psychologists over forty years ago, groupthink occurs when members of a group adhere to the same ideals and remain in agreement on all issues, despite the fact that most or all of the group are wrong in their assessment. They will make the same decision, even when that decision isn't the best. In a group study situation, groupthink might lead to faulty decision-making when it comes to choosing how best to structure sessions, or whether a particular interpretation of a theory is correct. Psychologists believe that groupthink arises when people prioritize harmony over accuracy and progress.

If you understand the factors that make a team more vulnerable to groupthink, you can prevent it occurring. Groupthink is more likely to develop when a group is lead by a charismatic, persuasive leader. **To ensure that no single individual takes over and subtly (or not so subtly) imposes their will and opinions, everyone should take it in turns to direct the group's activities.** A loose, ill-defined structure is another risk factor, because this invites universal agreement as a shortcut to closing on topic before moving onto the next. It is a good idea to take it turns to play devil's advocate.

For example, suppose one person has stated that they believe their interpretation of a philosophical theory to be correct. If they are particularly assertive, others may convince

---

[80] Janis, I.L. (1971). "Groupthink." *Psychology Today, 5, 6*, 43-46.

themselves that this individual is right, and everyone goes away from the group session with a flawed understanding of the topic. Assigning someone the role of devil's advocate for the duration of each study session is an effective way of preventing universal agreement for the sake of keeping the peace.

Whenever a group member makes a sweeping statement that goes unchallenged by others, the appointed advocate should step in and challenge them with questions that probe their thoughts and examine the quality of their arguments. This technique relies on all group members being able to handle constructive criticism, but if you have put together a group of sensible individuals, this should not be a problem.

On the other hand, you may find that arguments erupt from time to time. For example, two or more group members may disagree when it comes to understanding a piece of information under discussion. The fairest and quickest way of sorting out disputes is to ask your professor or TA. Email may be preferable to asking them in person, because then you will have a written record that can serve as the final verdict.

Finally, you need to be mindful when it comes to sharing notes, flashcards, and answers to practice exam questions. For the most part, it's a good idea to share notes – but this should be in addition to, not instead of, the individual study process. Do not assume that you are safe to skip the note-taking process for a couple of areas on the basis that someone else in your group promised to do it.

Why is it dangerous to trust that someone else will come through for you? For a start, they may be unwilling or unable to follow through on their promise. Second, even if they do supply you with their notes, there is no guarantee that they will make much sense to you. **Remember, we all have our own style when it comes to recording and making sense of information.** Just because you can understand your own unique shorthand system and abstract diagrams doesn't mean that your peers will be able to say the same.

You should also bear in mind that teachers and professors do not look kindly upon students who share one another's notes and produce near-identical exam answers as a result. If an examiner is grading two scripts that look alike, they will start to question whether one or both of you have cheated on the exam. In most cases, both parties are punished on the basis that it is impossible to ascertain for sure who copied whose notes. To avoid this scenario, avoid memorizing a study partner's notes word for word. Never use their answers to past exam questions as the basis of your own.

There is a fine line between using their notes to supplement your learning, and committing an act of blatant plagiarism. A comprehensive discussion of plagiarism and how to avoid it is beyond the scope of this book, but if you aren't sure whether your study techniques comply with the guidelines set down by your school or college, check with your student support center.

Although they can be difficult to establish and run, I'd recommend trying a study group. You might not start off as friends, but your study buddies might become members of your social circle within a few weeks! **Study groups are best suited for situations in which you have lots of time in which to prepare for an exam.** They are not as effective in high-stress situations in which you are faced with a major assessment in the upcoming days. **In these situations, the time it takes to put together a group and plan your sessions is time better spent studying.**

You may be wondering what you should be doing if you have an important test looming, but have yet to sit down and study for it. In the next chapter, I'll tell you precisely what you need to do in order to maximize your chances of passing, even if you have been skipping most of your lectures.

Chapter 20: How To Cram Before An Exam

Ideally, you will never have to cram the week or night before an exam, but most of us end up doing just that at one time or another. Whilst you stand a better chance of long-term success if you use the other techniques in this book, I realize that a chapter on effective cramming will probably help a few students! I'll share with you a rundown of what you should do with your last few precious study hours. **You might not get the best grade, but effective cramming can make the difference between passing and failing.** The method I'm about to share with you is partially based on my own experience in cramming before a history exam in college, and also on the advice given by GearFire blogger and student David Pierce.[81] Cramming is arguably the ultimate in accelerated learning techniques – if it works. As I'll explain later on in this chapter, I don't recommend it, but appreciate that it's necessary on occasion.

So, how should you start? Your attitude will determine how much progress you can make in the time you have available. When you have an important test coming up and you have barely opened a textbook or looked over your notes, you may feel as though you are defeated before you even begin. Choose to think about the situation in a new way. Yes, you made a mistake in delaying your revision, but this is a chance to prove to yourself that you can cope under pressure. Take a few deep breaths and put the situation into perspective – even if you fail the exam, it's unlikely to ruin your future. If you still catch yourself worrying, remember that no matter how worried you are, it won't change anything. **All you can do is to salvage the situation to the best of your ability.**

Once you've calmed down, your next step is to construct a realistic timetable. There is no point in trying to stay up all night to cram. When it comes to taking the test, you'll be too tired to function properly. Your brain needs time in which to consolidate new information. You absolutely must make time for sleeping, eating, and study breaks. Let's say you have 24 hours in which to prepare for a test. A sensible approach would be to begin by drawing up an hour-by-hour schedule that takes into account all of the above activities. **Don't overthink this step – ten minutes should be enough.** You don't have enough spare time to worry about making a pretty timetable! If possible, schedule the most difficult topics for the times of day you feel

---

[81] Pierce, D. (n.d.) *10 Ways to Cram Successfully*. http://www.gearfire.net/10-ways-cram-successfully/

most awake. Most of us perform best when we have been awake for two or three hours. At this point, you should be feeling slightly more relaxed.

Your next task is to make a list of the key points you need to cover. You don't have time to worry about the finer details or subtopics. Stick to the general points and overarching concepts. **Which topics get the most space in your textbook, receive the most attention from your professor, and come up on the practice test papers?** Skim through the opening and closing chapters of your textbooks, and pick out the key points from the summaries. This will give you an idea of the concepts you need to have in place in order to develop a basic understanding of the topic.

The good news is that you may know more than you think. The key is to quickly ascertain what you know, and then compensate for your deficiencies as fast as possible. Start by using practice papers. Under normal circumstances, you would use them to rehearse the skills you need to succeed in the real assessment, but if you are cramming, this exercise needs to be condensed into a shorter period of time. **Instead of writing out full answers, jot down the main ideas as bullet points.**

You won't benefit from the chance to practice structuring your answers, but you will gain valuable insight into the kind of questions you will be asked, which will at least remove some of the mystery surrounding the exam. You will also know, within a couple of hours, the areas in which you already have some knowledge. Take at least two practice tests if possible. If you are revising for a multiple-choice quiz, this step will take less time.

Based on the results of your trial exams, you will now be able to better prioritize the areas you need to study. How you do this is up to you, and depends on which of the techniques in this book are most appropriate to your situation. **You need to take into account the nature of the subject you are studying.** For example, if you need to memorize the names and population figures for a long list of cities, flashcards would work well. They allow you to quickly practice processing and recalling a lot of information within a relatively short space of time. If you needed to know how a biological or economic system works, the Feynman technique would be a better choice, as it provides you with more space in which to explore abstract concepts. If the subject is vast and contains many subtopics, mind mapping would be an effective means of condensing it all down onto a single sheet of paper.

After two to three hours of studying, return to your practice tests. This time around, you should feel more confident in approaching the questions. Compare your answers with those you produced during your initial attempt. **In which areas have you improved, and which material warrants further study?** Do not repeat the same study techniques over and over again if they are not working. You need to set up an efficient feedback loop that allows you to gain insight into your weak areas, develop your knowledge in short bursts of revision, test yourself again, and so on. Be proactive! Do not give in to feelings of helplessness. Make every minute count. **When you feel yourself becoming fatigued, it's time to take a break and eat a healthy snack in order to keep your blood sugar steady. Use the Pomodoro technique to ensure that you take regular breaks.**

Take a few notes with you on the morning or afternoon of the exam, and read over them just before entering the room. This won't help you absorb a lot of new information, but it may act as a prompt for recall. **As soon as the test begins, scribble down the key concepts on the bottom of the page, or on the back of the test.** You can always cross these notes out at the end. If you are writing an essay-style response, make sure that you draw a large cross through your notes so that they aren't graded by the examiner.

At this point, some of you may be shaking your heads. I know what you're thinking – you've probably crammed for an exam before, and done just fine. I admit that cramming is far from useless. In fact, there is research in support of cramming! For example, a major review of the topic concluded that it is beneficial for several reasons. It allows students to spend less time studying and more time on enjoyable activities, or other courses of study. For students who have fallen behind in class, it can compensate (to a degree) for their lack of prior knowledge.

Cramming can induce feelings of motivation, because the student knows that they are under great pressure. In a strange way, cramming also makes the study process more exciting. Most significant of all, there is little relationship between exam performance and length of a student's revision period, i.e. the time between the point at which they begin studying, and the date of the test.[82]

So why am I so anti-cramming? I maintain that it's a bad idea, for multiple reasons. **First of all, it's stressful.** The feeling you get when you realize how underprepared you are for a major exam is awful. Why put yourself through that torment? Exams are rarely fun, but the process is less traumatic when you don't have thoughts like *I'm going to fail, My grades will suck,* and even *My parents will be so mad!* whirring through your head. Worse, habitual cramming and the resulting stress will teach you to associate education and learning with unpleasant emotions. This means that you are less likely to seek out further training and formal education in later life.

Second, it sets you up for bad habits that will make your college and working life difficult. When you enter the workplace and need to complete important projects for other people, your boss won't be very impressed when they inevitably find out that you left everything until the last minute. Some people can get away with habitual procrastination, but most of us aren't so lucky. Chances are, if you make mistakes and are found to be a chronic procrastinator, you won't last long in your job.

Third, you'll never know how much better you could have done if you'd taken a long-term strategy, rather than waiting until the last minute and attempting to learn everything in a short space of time. Remember, research has proven the power of spaced repetition for long-term learning. Yes, you can stuff your head with information and recall it over the short term, but deep understanding comes only with practice and time. Cramming may offer some benefits, but research shows that the very best students play a long game. They study throughout the year, and they also study more intensively just prior to an assessment![83]

Cramming helps you learn information in a superficial way. **This allows you to pass exams, but good study habits will allow you to process it so that it becomes embedded in your long-term memory.** In psychology, this is termed "deeper learning," and is considered preferable because it is retained for a longer period of time. It also increases the likelihood that

---

[82] McIntyre, S.H., & Munson, J.M. (2008). Exploring Cramming: Student Behaviors, Beliefs, and Learning Retention in the Principles of Marketing Course. Journal of Marketing Education, 30, 226.
[83] Ibid.

you will be able to apply your knowledge across a broader range of contexts.

Finally, it's worth noting that the studies cited above do not account for the learning techniques used by crammers versus non-crammers. Neither do they account for individual differences. Cramming may work well for your friend or roommate, or even for the majority of students in one particular study, but why risk it when we know that successful students study on a regular basis and at an even pace? **Learn from the best. Adopt their strategies.**

Don't let yourself make a habit of cramming. **You are cheating yourself out of the chance to fulfil your potential.** If you find yourself resorting to cramming on a regular basis, it's time to reconsider your study habits, and perhaps your time management skills in general. The subject you are studying is another important factor. If you only need to learn facts for a test, cramming will produce better results than topics that require you to grasp complex concepts. It's always best to start studying as far in advance as possible. In the next chapter, we'll look at a type of skill that really needs to be built up over a long period of time in order to sink in – language.

Chapter 21: How To Learn A Language Fast

Language is a fundamental skill that we all have to learn. Right from birth, babies make cooing noises that form the basis of their first words. Within a couple of years, a young child will be using simple sentences, and expanding their vocabulary at an incredible rate. This all comes naturally, with little effort. Most of us acquire our native language with no explicit teaching, and are fully fluent by the age of five. If we want to learn an additional language after this point, we will need to make a conscious decision to acquire this new skill. In this chapter, I'll give you some practical tips and techniques from polyglots that will help you become fluent more quickly than you imagined possible!

Early on in this book, we looked at experiential learning and the power of immediate feedback. To briefly recap, an experiential approach is perfect when learning a language, because you receive instant feedback on your vocabulary, pronunciation, and grammar. For example, if you have regular conversations with a helpful native speaker, they will soon correct you when you go wrong. Their comments will set you on the right path, which will accelerate your learning.

The proven value of experiential learning is what makes language immersion techniques so popular. **However, immersion doesn't guarantee that someone will pick up a language.** For example, there are many English-speaking expat communities within various countries around the world. These communities are often made up of individuals who have no interest in learning the local language or culture. Often, they just want to live in a particular region, perhaps because they enjoy the climate.

Motivation makes all the difference. If you are not receptive to learning a new language, you won't make any progress. Polyglot Matthew Youlden, who speaks nine languages, believes that his high levels of motivation are a key driver behind his success. From the age of eight, Youlden and his twin brother Michael would attempt to learn new languages and be the first to gain proficiency. To this day, the brothers still spur each other on. Youlden believes that one of the best ways to learn a language is to find a partner who wants to learn it just as much – if not more – than you do.[84] A bit of healthy competition can work in your favor.

---

[84] Jordan, J. (2017). *10 Tips and Tricks To Learn Any Language.* https://www.babbel.com/en/magazine/10-tips-from-an-expert

Ask yourself why you are bothering to learn a language in the first place. Even though embarking on a new linguistic journey can be fun, and you should be able to acquire conversation-level proficiency within a few months, it requires hard work. If your ambition is to become fluent – particularly if you intend to read and write the language as well as speak it – you need to be clear as to your underlying goal. The type of reason you use will affect your chances of success.[85]

For example, if you are looking to learn Arabic in order to appear smart, you will be likely to run out of motivation quickly when encountering setbacks. On the other hand, let's say you wanted to learn Arabic in order to read ancient Arabic texts exactly as they were written. Knowing that you will be able to appreciate them more in their original form might excite you, and the feeling of anticipation may be enough to keep you going.

To use another example, suppose you learn that you have relatives in another country – and English isn't their first language. Your goal in learning to speak their language would be driven by the desire to form new relationships with your relatives, a powerful motive that will encourage you to keep going even when you struggle.

If you feel uneasy or even nervous about trying to learn a second language, you might be allowing negative beliefs to hold you back. If you let them go unchallenged, they will sap your motivation. Perhaps one of the most common misconceptions that people hold about language learning is that the older we get, the harder it is to learn another language. According to popular wisdom, children find it easy to learn a new language, teenagers find it more difficult, and those who have reached middle age may as well give up.

Not only is this belief depressing, it happens to be incorrect. A review published in the journal *Second Language Research* back in 1997 showed that age isn't a big factor in determining how easily someone will pick up another language.[86] **The primary factor is actually the degree to which the new language is similar in structure to a learner's**

---

[85] Ibid.
[86] Bialystok, E. (1997). The structure of age: In search of barriers to second language acquisition. *Second Language Research, 13*, 2.

native language. This is why Spanish is much easier for a native English speaker to learn compared to Arabic or Mandarin. The second most important factor is the length of time a learner has spent speaking their new language. Essentially, the more practice you put in, the better you can expect to become. If you were to visit language classes for adult learners (assuming you haven't already done so), you would see people of all ages mastering their second, third, or even fourth language.

Another belief that sets back new learners is the notion that if they are ever to attain a level of fluency sufficient to engage native speakers in conversation, they need to memorize hundreds of thousands of words. However, as lifestyle hacker and self-development guru Tim Ferriss points out, you don't need to know every word in a language in order to function as a fluent speaker. Even if you are a native speaker of English, it's unlikely that you know every word in an English dictionary. The Pareto Principle applies here – the majority of everyday conversation features only a relatively small number of words.[87]

As long as you correctly identify the most common words and devote your time to memorizing them, you will soon be able to converse on a number of everyday topics. If you are trying to learn a language alone, you may wonder where to start. However, there's no need to work out for yourself which words come up most often in everyday conversation. Go to any large online bookstore and search for "frequency dictionary + [your target language]."

Frequency dictionaries typically contain the most common 1,000-3,000 words, with a separate section for verbs. They may also contain pronunciation guidelines. When used in conjunction with immersion-style techniques such as watching a TV show in the target language or reading simple prose, they are useful tools that will allow you to pick up high-frequency words within a relatively short space of time.

Use flashcards to practice pieces of vocabulary. Many of the same principles you would use when studying other subjects apply here. For instance, you should stick to one word per card, and be sure to distinguish between recall and recognition. You can make your own

---

[87] Ferriss, T. (2014). 12 Rules for Learning Foreign Languages in Record Time – The Only Post You'll Ever Need. https://tim.blog/2014/03/21/how-to-learn-a-foreign-language-2/

flashcards using words you have come across, or words in your frequency dictionary. Alternatively, you can use an app designed to help you learn a language via virtual flashcards. I like AnkiApp, as it gives me access to thousands of flashcards, each fully customizable to suit my needs.

Youlden believes that it's important to set, and meet, realistic yet rewarding goals along the way as you learn a language. Remember what language is actually for – it allows two people to exchange ideas, interact, and share experiences. Base your goals around your original reasons for learning the language and what you hope to be able to do as you increase your proficiency.

For example, your ultimate goals might be to have a ten-minute conversation with a native Greek speaker and to understand every main feature in an edition of a Greek newspaper. **These are sensible and motivating goals, because they have a clearly defined end point, and having the capacity to talk to a native speaker and understand current affairs in their country are both useful skills.**

However, to go from knowing no Greek whatsoever to holding a full conversation with a native speaker would be overly ambitious. A more sensible approach would be to first set yourself the goal of being able to greet a fellow speaker before telling them your name. When it comes to reading a newspaper, a good initial goal would be to understand a headline without the need of a translator or dictionary. As a general rule, if you ever become discouraged, you need to set yourself simpler goals.

When it comes to learning new vocabulary, you can use a wide range of tools. Along with flashcards, mnemonic devices can also work if you are finding it hard to remember a word. For example, the French word for "dog" is "chien," pronounced "she-an." "Chien" resembles the word "chain," so you may find a mental image of a dog with a chain around its neck to be a useful mnemonic device. As with any other topic, tests and quizzes are among the best ways to consolidate new knowledge, and identify any weaknesses. There are many free online quizzes you can use to check your progress.

However, although these are a good resource when you need to refine your knowledge of grammar and the correct use of tenses, they are no substitute for the kind of experiential learning that comes with real-time practice. Take every opportunity you can to practice speaking your target language. Study groups are one of the best possible approaches to language learning. You could ask everyone to prepare to speak on a particular topic each week, and then form pairs during the study session. Each pair should try and hold a conversation on the topic for at least three minutes.

The difficulty and duration of the group exercises you use will depend on your proficiency, but the key principle is simple – everyone should be given the chance to practice with at least one other person, for at least several minutes at a time. If someone makes a mistake, they should receive feedback as soon as possible. Ideally, your study group should include a native speaker, whose role it is to offer guidance on vocabulary, grammar, and pronunciation.

A lot of learners find it hard to correctly pronounce new words. The quickest way to remedy this is not to repeat the same word over and over again in the hope that you get it right, but to watch someone else speak. Ideally, you'd be able to ask a native speaker to pronounce the word in front of you then correct you if necessary, but you can also refer to YouTube videos and footage of people in TV shows and movies.

Don't just focus on what they are saying – look at how their bodies move whilst they are saying it. How are they holding their faces and necks? What shape does their mouth make? **If you can accurately imitate their appearance, you stand a better chance of pronouncing the word correctly.**[88]

Once you have mastered the right pronunciation, use the word several times within your next few practice sessions. If you don't have anyone to talk to, either in person or online, why not try talking to yourself? It may seem a bit strange, but speaking words and phrases aloud rather than merely thinking about them will consolidate your learning and help you practice using them in conversation, even if it is a one-sided exchange.

As you go about your day, pretend that you are narrating your own actions. **In your target**

---

[88] Jordan, J. (2017). 10 Tips and Tricks To Learn Any Language. https://www.babbel.com/en/magazine/10-tips-from-an-expert

language, comment aloud on the time you woke up, what you did when you got out of bed, the clothes you put on, and so forth. You will feel self-conscious the first few times, but then you will come to realize how useful this exercise is. Not only will you be able to practice your pronunciation, but you will learn the words that matter most. When you talk through the mundane actions of your daily life, you'll see that the same words come up again and again. If you are struggling to translate the basics, such as "I ate…," then you will know exactly what you need to look up, and the areas in which you need to expand your vocabulary.

In summary, learning a new language can be difficult – but it is also immensely rewarding. It makes you feel as though you are a global citizen, and can open doors to new professional and personal opportunities. It can also be a lot of fun. **In fact, Youlden advises that if you can't have fun whilst learning a language, you have become too disengaged from the material and need to find a way of making it more interesting.** You could write a poem in your target language, for example, if doing so would make the prospect of revising vocabulary and grammar more appealing. In the next chapter, we'll look at another highly specific form of learning that becomes easier when you have tailor-made strategies at your disposal.

Chapter 22: Social Learning – How To Remember Names & Faces

Most of us think about learning in an academic context, but learning is a broad term that encompasses almost every area of our lives. In this chapter, we're going to look at social learning. Specifically, I'll teach you a few techniques that will allow you to remember the names and faces of people you meet. If you have ever spoken to someone on a couple of occasions and yet still found yourself unable to remember their name, you'll appreciate the value of this skill! When you remember someone else's name, they feel as though you must be paying attention to them, listening to what they have to say, and generally taking them seriously as a person. By extension, they will feel warmer towards you.

We'll start with names. When you next find yourself in a social situation, take a proactive approach when you have the chance to interact with other people. Don't just stand or sit there whilst waiting for someone to introduce you to a new person. Take a subtle look at their face, think about what kind of person they might be – in short, engage your brain. Ask yourself what you think their name might be in advance. This primes your brain to accept the information when it is finally offered.

The memory champion Ron White, who won the USA Memory Championship in 2009 and 2010, believes that people don't actually forget names – they just don't pay attention the first time they hear them.[89] **If you need an incentive to learn a name, take a pragmatic view and ask yourself what a good relationship with this person could mean for you.** If they are about to start as a new employee in your department, think about the alliance you could form as two colleagues in the workplace. If they are dating a member of your extended family, think about their potential as a future friend. If they are a potential client or business contact, think about the financial benefits that could come your way if you were to build a strong rapport with this person.

A lot of us feel nervous in social situations. We spend too much time thinking about hypothetical situations and what we might say next. **The problem is that these thoughts distract us from the person in front of us.** Before you know it, you've shaken someone's hand and

---

[89] Clifford, C. (2016). *11 memory hacks to remember the names of everyone you meet.* https://www.cnbc.com/2016/09/21/11-memory-hacks-to-remember-the-names-of-everyone-you-meet.html

made eye contact without having a clue as to what their name might be! **It may sound counterintuitive, but one of the most helpful social skills you can develop is the ability to be quiet, both in terms of what you say and in terms of what you think.** If you have a stream of internal chatter going on, you will miss out on everything that is happening around you. If you suffer from significant social anxiety or feel too self-conscious to remain calm around other people, consider a regular meditation practice, or even psychotherapy.

Once you have been formally introduced to someone, make full eye contact as you say their name aloud. Obviously, you need to do this in a natural manner. Say, "It's good to meet you [Name]," or "So you're [Name]! I've heard good things about you." This isn't just politeness. Taking two or three seconds to give their name your full attention increases the odds that you will commit it to memory. It also gives the other person an opportunity to correct you if you mispronounce it. Don't overuse their name in conversation, but if you can slip it in a couple more times in your initial meeting, it will definitely help you recall it at a later date.[90] They may suspect that you are intentionally trying to learn their name, but they are more likely to be flattered than offended! (Later, when you bid them farewell, seize the chance to use their name again.)

The next step is to link their name with someone or something you already know. For example, suppose you have just been introduced to a new colleague by the name of Susan. If you happened to work with another Susan, you could make a mental note that you have now worked with two Susans. **This link will improve your chances of retaining their name.** Depending on the context, it may even be possible to mention such links in conversation. Obviously, this is not always advisable. For instance, if a new person immediately reminds you of your ugly Uncle Joe, you should keep this revelation to yourself. Introducing someone else to your new acquaintance is another technique that cements their name in your memory.

Alliteration or nicknames also work well as a memory aid. **Challenge yourself to think of a new moniker for someone within five minutes of meeting them.** This nickname can be flattering, neutral, or even slightly rude. It doesn't matter, as long as they help you remember the person's name. Of course, you need to be careful not to let any unflattering nicknames slip

---

[90] Ibid.

out at an inconvenient moment.

After you have been introduced to a person and have learned their name, you need to work on committing their face to memory. One effective method is to discreetly scan their face and body, and locate their most distinguishing feature.[91] Needless to say, this will be easier in some cases than others. However, even the most average-looking person has something that sets them apart from other people you know. If they truly are unremarkable in every respect, that in itself is pretty memorable. Repeat their name in your mind as you hone in on their most conspicuous feature.

Along with a general memory of their face and a specific memory of their most notable feature, you also need to find a way of matching their name to their appearance in your mind. This creates a bridge between the information you have stored about their face, and the information you have stored about their name. For example, if you are introduced to someone called James Bridges, you could create a visual image of a man bending over in a bridge-like pose. This also works for first names. You can make use of rhymes or rhythms if their name doesn't immediately conjure up any powerful images. For example, let's say you have been introduced to a woman called Jane. "Jane" rhymes with "pane," so you might picture her face looking through a pane of glass.

Remember, spaced repetition is an effective means of committing information to long-term memory. Social learning is no exception to the rule. **If you need to learn several new names and faces – for example, if you have just started a new job, or are teaching a class of new students – test your memory for their names and faces every day.** If you are a teacher, for instance, write down as many of your students' names as possible after each class.

For each individual, bring to mind any distinguishing features. If you are a businessperson who needs to remember the names and faces of several people you just met at a large conference, take their business cards and write a few notes about their personality and physical appearance on the back of each. Keep them in a stack on your desk, and flick through them during quiet

---

[91] Ibid.

moments in the office. Think of them as your social flashcards.

Finally, talking about someone you have just met is an effective way of consolidating what you have just learned about them. If you have been to a conference, tell your colleagues who you met when you arrive back at the office. If you go to a large family party and meet your cousin's new boyfriend, tell your friend all about him when you next meet them for coffee. The more links you make between an individual and what you already know, the more likely you are to remember their name and face.

Chapter 23: Conclusion

By now, you'll have at your disposal a wide range of techniques that will supercharge your learning. Whether you are a college student studying for your final exams, a full-time parent wanting to improve their math skills so that you can help your child with their homework, or an executive fitting a part-time MBA around a packed schedule, you are now on the right track. In this chapter, I'm going to make a few suggestions as to how you can make the most of your new skills. **When you have learned how to learn, you are in a position to overhaul every aspect of your life!**

Hopefully, you'll have already seen the positive impact these techniques can have. **In writing this book, I hope to inspire people to take up skills and subjects they thought were "too difficult."** I also wanted to reach out to those who would like to go back to college or take up a workplace qualification, but feel themselves to be too old. You'll have noticed that none of the techniques in this book come with an upper age limit! If you have been contemplating a return to formal education, your new learning toolkit will put you in a strong position to succeed.

For those of you who are still in school, congratulations on taking your learning seriously at such a young age. **You'll know by now that it doesn't matter whether your IQ score is higher or lower than that of your peers – what really counts is your attitude, together with the methods you use when attempting to absorb new information.** If you have any friends who try hard to get good grades, yet persistently fail to increase their marks, encourage them to get a copy of this book.

If you are a parent, you can use this book to teach your children how to learn. You may not be an expert in any particular subject, but if you show them how to discover and retain new material for themselves, they will thank you later! Take an interest in the way they are taught at school. Do their teachers use an interactive learning style, or are students encouraged to learn material so that they can recite it on demand? If their teacher believes in the theory of learning styles, provide an alternative perspective at home. In age-appropriate language, explain that there isn't much proof that learning styles really exist, and there are better ways to think about learning. If you have the time and energy, consider challenging the school's position by writing a letter or even suggesting a parent-teacher consultation meeting. Your actions might benefit hundreds of children for years to come!

As soon as your child is old enough, ask them how they personally prefer to learn, and talk about whether their methods help them achieve their goals. **Remember that a child can prefer a method that doesn't actually help them learn.** Explain why some methods work better than others. Tell them why we sometimes have to think about what will work, rather than what we would most like to do. Encourage them to make a study timetable as soon as it becomes necessary, and make sure they understand the importance of scheduling in some recreational activities alongside their learning periods. Getting good study habits in place in their early years will provide a solid foundation for achievement in high school and college. Do not rely on your child's school to train them how to learn.

Older children and teenagers will benefit from many of the methods outlined in this book, so pass it on to them if they are old enough to understand it. Bear in mind that they may not want or need to use all of the techniques listed here, and that's perfectly OK. Young teenagers in particular often pass through a rebellious phase. During this period, they may not want to study at all. Even if you were to chain them to a desk with a stack of textbooks in front of them, you can't make a teen learn against their will. **However, you can gently suggest that developing a few accelerated learning techniques can help them achieve better grades whilst working smarter rather than harder.** That might provide them with the incentive they need to at least give some of these ideas a try!

If you happen to be a teacher or educator, why not pass on these skills to your students? I have included citations throughout the book, which will act as a good starting point if you would like to research these ideas further. If you are teaching a class on education, teaching, psychology, or another allied discipline, then you are in an excellent position to spread the ideas contained within these chapters. **Set aside at least a couple of hours every term to talk about learning – what it is, the ways in which people learn best, and so on.**

Ask students for their honest feedback. How could you present information in a way that makes the most sense to them? You don't have to take their suggestions on board, but it can be illuminating to discover what they think of your teaching style, and how they believe the learning process to work. You can make this feedback process anonymous if you suspect that they might withhold their opinions for fear of getting into trouble.

Does your job entail managing other people in the workplace? If so, this book should have given you some insight into why some people seem more competent than others, and why some individuals may be struggling in their roles. Of course, each situation will be different, but there are some general principles you can take away and implement at work. For example, if you are uncertain as to whether someone in your team really understands what you have asked them to do, employ the Feynman technique and request that they explain the task to you in their own words. **You will quickly spot any gaps in their understanding.**

The chapter on learning in groups will be useful if you oversee group projects, as it outlines the ways in which social dynamics can undermine everyone's learning experience. If you think that a particular technique might benefit your colleagues, why not suggest a learning and development session based around some of the chapters in this book?

Having discovered more about the ways in which people learn, you might be more willing to accommodate team members who are in need of a little extra help or reasonable adjustments. For example, perhaps one of your team could benefit from soothing ambient noise in order to drown out the background chatter of the office if they are currently working on a complex project.

If you are in a position to do so, you may wish to give employees the option of using standing desks. Depending on the size of your team, giving everyone this choice may not be financially viable, but you could introduce a hot-desking system or allow workers to set up their own standing desks in the office. This option may not only improve their productivity, but also provide them with a sense of choice, which furthers a sense of autonomy and increases morale.

Meta-learning – learning how to learn – is one of the most useful skills you can acquire. Best of all, you can practice your learning techniques in many different contexts over the course of your life. However you decide to apply these techniques, I wish you good luck in growing your skills and expanding your knowledge. Have fun!

<u>**One last thing before you go. Can I ask you a favor? I need your help!**</u>
If you enjoyed this book, could you please share your experience on Amazon and

write an honest review? It will be just one minute of your time (I will be happy even with one sentence!), but a GREAT help for me and definitely a good Karma ;)

Since I'm not a well-established author and I don't have powerful people and big publishing companies supporting me, I read every single review and jump around with joy like a little kid every time my readers comment on one of my books and give me their honest feedback! If I was able to inspire you in any way, please let me know! It will also help me get my books in front of more people looking for new ideas and useful knowledge.

If you did not enjoy the book or had a problem with it, please don't hesitate to contact me at contact@mindfulnessforsuccess.com and tell me how I can improve it to provide more value and more knowledge to my readers. I'm constantly working on my books to make them better and more helpful.

Thank you and good luck! I believe in you and I wish you all the best on your new journey!
Your friend,
Ian

My Free Gift to You – Get One of My Audiobooks For Free!

If you've never created an account on Audible (the biggest audiobook store in the world), **you can claim one free** audiobook **of mine**!

It's a simple process:

1. Pick one of my audiobooks on Audible:
http://www.audible.com/search?advsearchKeywords=Ian+Tuhovsky
Shortened link: http://tinyurl.com/IanTuhovskyAudiobooks
2. Once you choose a book and open its detail page, click the orange button "Free with 30-Day Trial Membership."
3. Follow the instructions to create your account and download your first free audiobook.

Note that you are NOT obligated to continue after your free trial expires. You can cancel your free trial easily anytime and you won't be charged at all.

Also, if you haven't downloaded your free book already:

Discover How to Get Rid of Stress & Anxiety and Reach Inner Peace in 20 Days or Less!

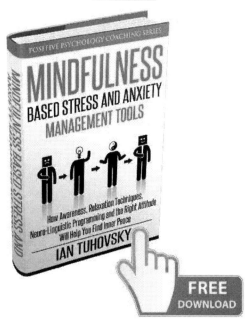

To help speed up your personal transformation, I have prepared a special gift for you!

Download my full, 120 page e-book "Mindfulness Based Stress and Anxiety Management Tools" for free by clicking here.

Link:

tinyurl.com/mindfulnessgift

Hey there like-minded friends, let's get connected!

Don't hesitate to visit:
-My Blog: www.mindfulnessforsuccess.com
-My Facebook fanpage: https://www.facebook.com/mindfulnessforsuccess
-My Instagram profile: https://instagram.com/mindfulnessforsuccess
-My Amazon profile: amazon.com/author/iantuhovsky

Recommended Reading for You:

If you are interested in Self-Development, Psychology, Social Dynamics, PR, Soft Skills, Spirituality and related topics, you might be interested in previewing or downloading my other books:

Self-Discipline: Mental Toughness Mindset: Increase Your Grit and Focus to Become a Highly Productive (and Peaceful!) Person

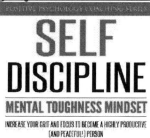

This Mindset and Exercises Will Help You Build Everlasting Self-Discipline and Unbeatable Willpower

Imagine that you have this rare kind of power that enables you to maintain iron resolve, crystal clarity, and everyday focus to gradually realize all of your dreams by consistently ticking one goal after another off your to-do list.

Way too often, people and their minds don't really play in one team.
Wouldn't that be profoundly life-changing to utilize that power to make the best partners with your brain?

This rare kind of power is a mindset. The way you think, the way you perceive and handle both the world around you and your inner reality, will ultimately determine the quality of your life.

A single shift in your perception can trigger meaningful results.

Life can be tough. Whenever we turn, there are obstacles blocking our way. Some are caused by our environment, and some by ourselves. Yet, we all know people who are able to overcome them consistently, and, simply speaking, become successful. And stay there!

What really elevates a regular Joe or Jane to superhero status is the laser-sharp focus, perseverance, and the ability to keep on going when everyone else would have quit.
I have, for a long time, studied the lives of the most disciplined people on this planet. In this book, you are going to learn their secrets.
No matter if your goals are financial, sport, relationship, or habit-changing oriented, this book covers it all.

Today, I want to share with you the science-based insights and field-tested methods that have helped me, my friends, and my clients change their lives and become real-life go-getters.

Here are some of the things you will learn from this book:

• **What the "positive thinking trap" means,** and how exactly should you use the power of positivity to actually help yourself instead of holding yourself back?
• What truly makes us happy and how does that relate to success? Is it money? Social position? Friends, family? Health? **No. There's actually something bigger, deeper, and much more fundamental behind our happiness.** You will be surprised to find out what the factor that ultimately drives us and keeps us going is, and this discovery can greatly improve your life.
• **Why our Western perception of both happiness and success are fundamentally wrong**, and how those misperceptions can kill your chances of succeeding?
• **Why relying on willpower and motivation is a very bad idea, and what to hold on to instead?** This is as important as using only the best gasoline in a top-grade sports car. Fill its engine with a moped fuel and keep the engine oil level low, and it won't get far. Your mind is this sports car engine. I will show you where to get this quality fuel from.
• **You will learn what the common denominator of the most successful and disciplined people on this planet is** – Navy SEALS and other special forces, Shaolin monks, top performing CEOs and Athletes, they, in fact, have a lot in common. I studied their lives for a long time, and now, it's time to share this knowledge with you.
• Why your entire life can be viewed as a piece of training, and **what are the rules of this training?**
• What the XX-th century Russian Nobel-Prize winner and long-forgotten genius Japanese psychotherapist **can teach you about the importance of your emotions and utilizing them correctly in your quest to becoming a self-disciplined and a peaceful person?**
• How modern science can help you **overcome temptation and empower your will**, and why following strict and inconvenient diets or regimens can actually help you achieve your goals in the end?
• How can you win by failing and **why giving up on some of your goals can actually be a good thing?**
• How do we often become **our own biggest enemies** in achieving our goals and how to finally change it?
• How to **maintain** your success once you achieve it?

Direct Buy Link to Amazon Kindle Store:
http://tinyurl.com/IanMentalToughness
Paperback version on Createspace: http://tinyurl.com/IanMTPaperback

Emotional Intelligence Training: A Practical Guide to Making Friends with Your Emotions and Raising Your EQ

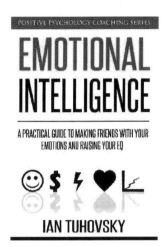

Do you believe your life would be healthier, happier and even better, if you had more practical strategies to regulate your own emotions?
Most people agree with that.
Or, more importantly:
Do you believe you'd be healthier and happier if everyone who you live with had the strategies to regulate their emotions?

...Right?

The truth is not too many people actually realize what EQ is really all about and what causes its popularity to grow constantly.

Scientific research conducted by many American and European universities prove that the **"common" intelligence responses account for less than 20% of our life achievements and successes, while the other over 80% depends on emotional intelligence.** To put it roughly: **either you are emotionally intelligent, or you're doomed to mediocrity, at best.**
As opposed to the popular image, emotionally intelligent people are not the ones who react impulsively and spontaneously, or who act lively and fiery in all types of social environments. Emotionally intelligent people are open to new experiences, can show feelings adequate to the situation, either good or bad, and find it easy to socialize with other people and establish new contacts. They handle stress well, say "no" easily, realistically assess the achievements of themselves or others and are not afraid of constructive criticism and taking calculated risks. **They are the people of success.** Unfortunately, this perfect model of an emotionally intelligent person is extremely rare in our modern times.

Sadly, nowadays, **the amount of emotional problems in the world is increasing at an alarming rate.** We are getting richer, but less and less happy. Depression, suicide, relationship breakdowns, loneliness of choice, fear of closeness, addictions—this is clear evidence that we are getting increasingly worse when it comes to dealing with our emotions. **Emotional intelligence is a SKILL, and can be learned through constant practice and training, just like riding a bike or swimming!**

This book is stuffed with lots of effective exercises, helpful info and practical ideas. Every chapter covers different areas of emotional intelligence and shows you, **step by step**, what exactly you can do to **develop your EQ** and become the **better version of yourself**. I will show you how freeing yourself from the domination of left-sided brain thinking can contribute to your inner transformation—**the emotional revolution that will help you redefine who you are and what you really want from life!**

In This Book I'll Show You:

- What Is Emotional Intelligence and What Does EQ Consist of?
- How to **Observe and Express** Your Emotions
- How to **Release Negative Emotions** and **Empower the Positive Ones**
- How to Deal with Your **Internal Dialogues**
- How to **Deal with the Past**
- **How to Forgive** Yourself and How to Forgive Others
- How to Free Yourself from **Other People's Opinions and Judgments**
- What Are "Submodalities" and How Exactly You Can Use Them to **Empower Yourself** and **Get Rid of Stress**
- The Nine Things You Need to **Stop Doing to Yourself**
- How to Examine Your Thoughts
- **Internal Conflicts** Troubleshooting Technique
- The Lost Art of Asking Yourself the Right Questions and **Discovering Your True Self!**
- How to Create Rich Visualizations
- LOTS of practical exercises from the mighty arsenal of psychology, family therapy, NLP etc.
- **And many, many more!**

Direct Buy Link to Amazon Kindle Store:
https://tinyurl.com/IanEQTrainingKindle
Paperback version on Createspace: https://tinyurl.com/ianEQpaperback

Communication Skills Training: A Practical Guide to Improving Your Social Intelligence, Presentation, Persuasion and Public Speaking

Do You Know How To Communicate With People Effectively, Avoid Conflicts and Get What You Want From Life?

...It's not only about what you say, but also about WHEN, WHY and HOW you say it.

Do The Things You Usually Say Help You, Or Maybe Hold You Back?

Have you ever considered **how many times you intuitively felt that maybe you lost something important or crucial, simply because you unwittingly said or did something, which put somebody off?** Maybe it was a misfortunate word, bad formulation, inappropriate joke, forgotten name, huge misinterpretation, awkward conversation or a strange tone of your voice?
Maybe you assumed that you knew exactly what a particular concept meant for another person and you stopped asking questions?
Maybe you could not listen carefully or could not stay silent for a moment? **How many times have you wanted to achieve something, negotiate better terms, or ask for a promotion and failed miserably?**

It's time to put that to an end with the help of this book.

<u>Lack of communication skills is exactly what ruins most peoples' lives.</u>
If you don't know how to communicate properly, you are going to have problems both in your intimate and family relationships.

You are going to be ineffective in work and business situations. It's going to be troublesome managing employees or getting what you want from your boss or your clients on a daily basis. Overall, **effective communication is like an engine oil which makes your life run smoothly, getting you wherever you want to be.** There are very few areas in life in which you can succeed in the long run without this crucial skill.

What Will You Learn With This Book?

-What Are The **Most Common Communication Obstacles** Between People And How To Avoid Them
-How To Express Anger And Avoid Conflicts
-What Are **The Most 8 Important Questions You Should Ask Yourself** If You Want To Be An Effective Communicator?
-**5 Most Basic and Crucial** Conversational Fixes
-How To Deal With Difficult and Toxic People
-Phrases to **Purge from Your Dictionary** (And What to Substitute Them With)
-The Subtle Art of **Giving and Receiving Feedback**
-Rapport, the **Art of Excellent Communication**
-How to Use Metaphors to **Communicate Better** And **Connect With People**
-What Metaprograms and Meta Models Are and How Exactly To Make Use of Them To **Become A Polished Communicator**
-How To Read Faces and **How to Effectively Predict Future Behaviors**
-How to Finally Start **Remembering Names**
-How to Have a Great Public Presentation
-How To Create Your Own **Unique Personality** in Business (and Everyday Life)
-Effective Networking

Direct link to Amazon Kindle Store: https://tinyurl.com/IanCommSkillsKindle

Paperback version on Createspace:
http://tinyurl.com/iancommunicationpaperback

Empath: An Empowering Book for the Highly Sensitive Person on Utilizing Your Unique Ability and Maximizing Your Human Potential

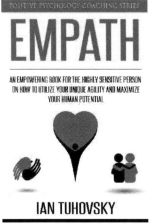

Have others ever told you to "stop being so sensitive?" Have you ever looked at other people and wondered how they manage to get through the day without noticing the suffering going on all around them?

Do you feel so emotionally delicate in comparison to your peers that you have tried to block out what is going on around you? You may have even resorted to coping mechanisms such as overeating, overworking, or smoking as a means of managing your emotions.

Maybe you have tried to "grow a thicker skin," or attempted to cover up your feelings with humor? Perhaps you have always felt different to others since childhood, but could never quite put your finger on why.

If this description resonates with you, congratulations! You may well be an Empath. **Unfortunately, an Empath who lacks insight into their own nature is likely to be miserable.**

Most of us are familiar with the concept of empathy. Aside from sociopaths, who are largely incapable of appreciating what another individual may be feeling, humans are generally able to understand what others are going through in most situations.
Empaths, however, constitute the small group of people who not only understand the emotions of others, but literally feel them too.

In short, an Empath takes this common human ability of relating to other peoples' emotions to extremes.

If you have no idea why you are so readily affected by the emotions of others and the events around you, you will become psychologically unstable. You will be unsure as to where your true feelings end, and those of other people begin.

Hypersensitivity can be a burden if not properly managed, which is why it's so important that all Empaths learn to harness the special gift they have been given. That's where this book comes in. Millions of other people around the world share your gifts and lead happy, fulfilling lives. Make no mistake – the world needs us.

It's time to learn how to put your rare gift to use, maximize your human potential, and thrive in life!

If you think you (or anyone around you) might be an Empath or the Highly Sensitive Person – this book is written for you.

<u>**What you will learn from this book:**</u>
-**What it really means to be an Empath** and the science behind the "Empath" and "the Highly Sensitive Person" classification. Find out how our brains work and why some people are way more sensitive than others.
-**What are the upsides of being an Empath** – find your strengths and thrive while making the most of your potential and providing value to this world (it NEEDS Empaths!) by making it a better place.
-**What are the usual problems that sensitive people struggle** with – overcome them by lessening the impact that other people's emotions and actions have on you, while still being truthful to your true nature, and learn how to take care of your mental health.
-**The great importance of becoming an emotionally intelligent person** – learn what EQ is and how you can actively develop it to become much more peaceful, effective, and a happy person. Discover the strategies that will help you stay balanced and be much more immune to the everyday struggles.
-**The workplace and career choices** – realize what you should be aware of and find how to make sure you don't stumble into the most common problems that sensitive people often fall prey to.
-**How to effectively handle conflicts, negative people, and toxic** relationships – since sensitive people are more much more immune to difficult relations and often become an easy target for those who tend to take advantage of others – it's time to put this to an end with this book.
-**How to deal with Empaths and Highly Sensitive People as a non-Empath** and what to focus on if you think that your kid might fall under this classification.
-**How to connect with other Empaths**, what is the importance of gender in this context, and how to stay in harmony with your environment – **you will learn all of this and more from this book!**

Direct Buy Link to Amazon Kindle Store:
http://tinyurl.com/IanEmpathKindle

Paperback version on Createspace:
http://tinyurl.com/IanEmpathPaperback

Confidence: Your Practical Training: How to Develop Healthy Self Esteem and Deep Self Confidence to Be Successful and Become True Friends with Yourself

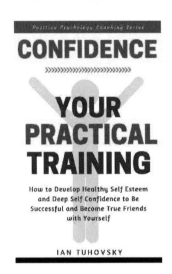

Have you ever considered how many opportunities you have missed and how many chances you have wasted by lacking self-confidence when you need it most?
Have you ever given up on your plans, important goals, and dreams not because you just decided to focus on something else, but simply because you were too SCARED or hesitant to even start, or stick up to the plan and keep going?

Are you afraid of starting your own business or asking for a promotion? Petrified of public speaking, socializing, dating, taking up new hobbies, or going to job interviews?

Can you imagine how amazing and relieving it would feel to finally obtain all the self-esteem needed to accomplish things you've always wanted to achieve in your life?

Finally, have you ever found yourself in a situation where you simply couldn't understand **WHY you acted in a certain way**, or why you kept holding yourself back and feeling all the bad emotions, instead of just going for what's the most important to you?

Due to early social conditioning and many other influences, most people on this planet are already familiar with all these feelings.

WAY TOO FAMILIAR!

I know how it feels, too. I was in the same exact place.

And then, I found the way!
It's high time you did something about it too because, truth be told, self-confident people just have it way easier in every single aspect of life!

From becoming your own boss or succeeding in your career, through dating and socializing, to starting new hobbies, standing up for yourself or maybe finally packing your suitcase and going on this Asia trip you promised yourself decades ago... All too often, people fail in these quests as they aren't equipped with the natural and lasting self-confidence to deal with them in a proper way.

Confidence is not useful only in everyday life and casual situations. Do you really want to fulfill your wildest dreams, or do you just want to keep chatting about them with your friends, until one day you wake up as a grumpy, old, frustrated person?
Big achievements require brave and fearless actions. If you want to act bravely, you need to be confident.

Along with lots of useful, practical exercises, this book will provide you with plenty of new information that will help you understand what confidence problems really come down to. And this is the most important and the saddest part, because most people do not truly recognize the root problem, and that's why they get poor results.

Lack of self-confidence and problems with unhealthy self-esteem are usually the reason why smart, competent, and talented people never achieve a satisfying life; a life that should easily be possible for them.

In this book, you will read about:
-How, when, and why society robs us all of natural confidence and healthy self-esteem.
-What kind of social and psychological traps you need to avoid in order to feel much calmer, happier, and more confident.
-What "natural confidence" means and how it becomes natural.
-What "self-confidence" really is and what it definitely isn't (as opposed to what most people think!).
-How your mind hurts you when it really just wants to help you, and how to stop the process.
-What different kinds of fear we feel, where they come from, and how to defeat them.
-How to have a great relationship with yourself.
-How to use stress to boost your inner strength.
-Effective and ineffective ways of building healthy self-esteem.
-Why the relation between self-acceptance and stress is so crucial.
-How to stay confident in professional situations.
-How to protect your self-esteem when life brings you down, and how to deal with criticism and jealousy.
-How to use neuro-linguistic programming, imagination, visualizations, diary entries, and your five senses to re-program your subconscious and get rid of "mental viruses" and detrimental beliefs that actively destroy your natural confidence and healthy self-esteem.
Take the right action and start changing your life for the better today!

DOWNLOAD FOR FREE from Amazon Kindle Store:
https://tinyurl.com/IanConfidenceTraining
Paperback version on Createspace:
http://tinyurl.com/IanConfidencePaperbackV

Mindfulness: The Most Effective Techniques: Connect With Your Inner Self to Reach Your Goals Easily and Peacefully

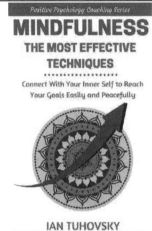

Mindfulness is not about complicated and otherworldly woo-woo spiritual practices. It doesn't require you to be a part of any religion or a movement.

What mindfulness is about is living a good life (that's quite practical, right?), and this book is all about deepening your awareness, **getting to know yourself**, and developing attitudes and mental habits that will make you not only a successful and effective person in life, but a happy and wise one as well.

If you have ever wondered what the mysterious words "mindfulness" means and why would anyone bother, you have just found your (detailed) answer!

This book will provide you with actionable steps and valuable information, all in plain English, so all of your doubts will be soon gone.

In my experience, **nothing has proven as simple and yet effective and powerful as the daily practice of mindfulness.**

It has helped me become more decisive, disciplined, focused, calm, and just a happier person.

I can come as far as to say that mindfulness has transformed me into a success.

Now, it's your turn.
There's nothing to lose, and so much to win!

The payoff is nothing less than transforming your life into its true potential.

What you will learn from this book:

-What exactly does the word "mindfulness" mean, and why should it become an important word in your dictionary?

-How taking **as little as five minutes a day** to clear your mind might result in steering your life towards great success and becoming a much more fulfilled person? ...and **how the heck can you "clear your mind" exactly?**

-What are the **most interesting, effective, and not well-known mindfulness techniques for success** that I personally use to stay on the track and achieve my goals daily while feeling calm and relaxed?

-**Where to start** and how to slowly get into mindfulness to avoid unnecessary confusion?

-What are the **scientifically proven profits** of a daily mindfulness practice?

-**How to develop the so-called "Nonjudgmental Awareness"** to win with discouragement and negative thoughts, **stick to the practice** and keep becoming a more focused, calm, disciplined, and peaceful person on a daily basis?

-What are **the most common problems** experienced by practitioners of mindfulness and meditation, and how to overcome them?

-How to meditate and **just how easy** can it be?

-What are **the most common mistakes** people keep doing when trying to get into meditation and mindfulness? How to avoid them?

-**Real life tested steps** to apply mindfulness to everyday life to become happier and much more successful person?

-What is the relation between mindfulness and life success? How to use mindfulness to become much more effective in your life and achieve your goals much easier?

-**What to do in life** when just about everything seems to go wrong?

-How to become a **more patient and disciplined person**?

Stop existing and start living.
Start changing your life for the better today.

DOWNLOAD FOR FREE from Amazon Kindle Store:

myBook.to/IanMindfulnessGuide
Paperback version on Createspace:

http://tinyurl.com/IanMindfulnessGuide

Meditation for Beginners: How to Meditate (as an Ordinary Person!) to Relieve Stress and Be Successful

Meditation doesn't have to be about crystals, hypnotic folk music and incense sticks! **Forget about sitting in unnatural and uncomfortable positions while going, "Ommmmm...."** It is not necessarily a club full of yoga masters, Shaolin monks, hippies and new-agers.

It is a super useful and universal practice which can improve your overall brain performance and happiness. When meditating, you take a step back from actively thinking your thoughts, and instead see them for what they are. The reason why meditation is helpful in reducing stress and attaining peace is that it gives your over-active consciousness a break.

Just like your body needs it, your mind does too!

I give you the gift of peace that I was able to attain through present moment awareness.

Direct Buy Link to Amazon Kindle Store:

https://tinyurl.com/IanMeditationGuide

Paperback version on Createspace: http://tinyurl.com/ianmeditationpaperback

Zen: Beginner's Guide: Happy, Peaceful and Focused Lifestyle for Everyone

Contrary to popular belief, Zen is not a discipline reserved for monks practicing Kung Fu. Although there is some truth to this idea, Zen is a practice that is applicable, useful and pragmatic for anyone to study regardless of what religion you follow (or don't follow).

Zen is the practice of studying your subconscious and **seeing your true nature.** The purpose of this work is to show you how to apply and utilize the teachings and essence of Zen in everyday life in the Western society. I'm not really an "absolute truth seeker" unworldly type of person—I just believe in practical plans and blueprints that actually help in living a better life. Of course I will tell you about the origin of Zen and the traditional ways of practicing it, but I will also show you my side of things, my personal point of view and translation of many Zen truths into a more "contemporary" and practical language.
It is a "modern Zen lifestyle" type of book.

What You Will Read About:
• Where Did Zen Come from? - A short history and explanation of Zen
• What Does Zen Teach? - The major teachings and precepts of Zen
• Various Zen meditation techniques that are applicable and practical for everyone!
• The Benefits of a Zen Lifestyle
• What Zen Buddhism is NOT?
• How to Slow Down and Start Enjoying Your Life
• How to Accept Everything and Lose Nothing
• Why Being Alone Can Be Beneficial
• Why Pleasure Is NOT Happiness
• Six Ways to Practically Let Go
• How to De-clutter Your Life and Live Simply
• "Mindfulness on Steroids"
• How to Take Care of Your Awareness and Focus
• Where to Start and How to Practice Zen as a Regular Person
• And many other interesting concepts...

I invite you to take this journey into the peaceful world of Zen Buddhism with me today!
Direct Buy Link to Amazon Kindle Store: https://tinyurl.com/IanZenGuide
Paperback version on Createspace: http://tinyurl.com/IanZenPaperbackV

Buddhism: Beginner's Guide: Bring Peace and Happiness to Your Everyday Life

Buddhism is one of the most practical and simple belief systems on this planet, and it has greatly helped me on my way to become a better person in every aspect possible. In this book I will show you what happened and how it was.

No matter if you are totally green when it comes to Buddha's teachings or maybe you have already heard something about them—this book will help you systematize your knowledge and will inspire you to learn more and to take steps to make your life positively better!

I invite you to take this beautiful journey into the graceful and meaningful world of Buddhism with me today!

Direct link to Amazon Kindle Store: https://tinyurl.com/IanBuddhismGuide
Paperback version on Createspace: http://tinyurl.com/ianbuddhismpaperback

About The Author

Author's blog: www.mindfulnessforsuccess.com
Author's Amazon profile: amazon.com/author/iantuhovsky
Instagram profile: https://instagram.com/mindfulnessforsuccess

Hi! I'm Ian...

. . . and I am interested in life. I am in the study of having an awesome and passionate life, which I believe is within the reach of practically everyone. I'm not a mentor or a guru. I'm just a guy who always knew there was more than we are told. I managed to turn my life around from way below my expectations to a really satisfying one, and now I want to share this fascinating journey with you so that you can do it, too.

I was born and raised somewhere in Eastern Europe, where Polar Bears eat people on the streets, we munch on snow instead of ice cream and there's only vodka instead of tap water, but since I make a living out of several different businesses, I move to a new country every couple of months. I also work as an HR consultant for various European companies.

I love self-development, traveling, recording music and providing value by helping others. I passionately read and write about social psychology, sociology, NLP, meditation, mindfulness, eastern philosophy, emotional intelligence, time management, communication skills and all of the topics related to conscious self-development and being the most awesome version of yourself.

Breathe. Relax. Feel that you're alive and smile. And never hesitate to contact me!

Made in the USA
Middletown, DE
25 November 2019